OFFICIATING TRACK & FIELD AND CROSS COUNTRY

A publication for the National Federation of State High School Associations Officials Education Program

Developed by the American Sport Education Program

Human Kinetics

Library of Congress Cataloging-in-Publication Data

American Sport Education Program.
  Officiating track & field and cross country / developed by the American Sport Education Program.
    p. cm.
  "A publication for the National Federation of State High School Associations Officials Education Program."
  Includes index.
  ISBN 0-7360-5360-3 (soft cover)
  1. Track and field--Officiating   2. Track and field--Rules.   I. Title: Officiating track & field and cross country.   II. National Federation of State High School Associations Officials Education Program.   III. Title.
  GV1060.5.A44 2006
  796.42--dc22
                                                                                2005008058

ISBN: 0-7360-5360-3

Copyright © 2006 by Human Kinetics, Inc.

The Web addresses cited in this text were current as of May 2005, unless otherwise noted.

NFHS Officials Education Program Coordinator: Mary Struckhoff; **Project Consultant:** Cynthia Doyle; **Project Writer:** Thomas Hanlon; **Acquisitions Editors:** Amy Tocco and Greg George; **Developmental Editor:** Laura Floch; **Assistant Editor:** Mandy Maiden; **Copyeditor:** John Wentworth; **Proofreader:** Sue Fetters; **Indexers:** Robert and Cynthia Swanson; **Graphic Designer:** Andrew Tietz; **Graphic Artist:** Sandra Meier; **Photo Manager:** Dan Wendt; **Cover Designer:** Jack W. Davis; **Photographer (cover):** Dan Wendt; **Photographer (interior):** Dan Wendt unless otherwise noted; photos on pages 45 and 53 (upper right) courtesy Sarah Ritz; photos on pages 78 and 79 courtesy Gill Athletics; photos on pages 1, 5, 8, 17, 31, 39, 97, 100, 106, 110, 113, 118, and 120 © Human Kinetics; **Art Manager:** Kareema McLendon-Foster; **Illustrators:** Argosy and Kareema McLendon-Foster; **Printer:** United Graphics

We thank Bloomington High School in Bloomington, Illinois, for assistance in providing the location for the photo shoot for this book.

Copies of this book are available at special discounts for bulk purchase for sales promotions, premiums, fundraising, or educational use. Special editions or book excerpts can also be created to specifications. For details, contact the Special Sales Manager at Human Kinetics.

Printed in the United States of America   10 9 8 7 6 5 4 3 2 1

Human Kinetics
Web site: www.HumanKinetics.com

United States: Human Kinetics
P.O. Box 5076, Champaign, IL 61825-5076
800-747-4457
e-mail: humank@hkusa.com

Canada: Human Kinetics
475 Devonshire Road Unit 100
Windsor, ON N8Y 2L5
800-465-7301 (in Canada only)
e-mail: orders@hkcanada.com

Europe: Human Kinetics
107 Bradford Road, Stanningley
Leeds LS28 6AT, United Kingdom
+44 (0) 113 255 5665
e-mail: hk@hkeurope.com

Australia: Human Kinetics
57A Price Avenue
Lower Mitcham, South Australia 5062
08 8277 1555
e-mail: liaw@hkaustralia.com

New Zealand: Human Kinetics
Division of Sports Distributors NZ Ltd.
P.O. Box 300 226 Albany
North Shore City, Auckland
0064 9 448 1207
e-mail: info@humankinetics.co.nz

CONTENTS

PREFACE

It's no secret that officials play essential roles in track and field and cross country. But how do officials come to know their stuff? How do they keep all the rules and mechanics straight? Educational tools and reference materials—such as this book—are important for all officials to learn their craft and stay sharp. *Officiating Track & Field and Cross Country* is a key resource for you if you want to officiate track and field meets and cross country meets at the high school level. The mechanics you'll find here are those developed by the National Federation of State High School Associations (NFHS) and are used for high school track and field meets and cross country meets throughout the United States.

We expect that you know at least a little about track and field and cross country, but maybe not much about officiating it. On the other end of the spectrum, you might know a great deal about the sports themselves and how to officiate them. But the overall objective of *Officiating Track & Field and Cross Country* is to prepare you to officiate meets, no matter what your level of experience. More specifically, this book should

- introduce you to the culture of officiating,
- tell you what will be expected of you as an official,
- explain and illustrate the mechanics of officiating in detail,
- show connection between the rules and the mechanics of officiating them, and
- serve as a reference for you throughout your officiating career.

Officiating Track & Field and Cross Country covers officiating basics of the sports, officiating mechanics and specific meet situations. In part I, you'll read about who track and field and cross country officials are and what kinds of qualities you'll find in a good official. Part I also describes meet responsibilities, including premeet, prerace and race duties. Part II, the meat of the book, describes mechanics in careful detail. Part III highlights some key cases from the NFHS *Track and Field and Cross Country Case Book* and shows how you, the official, apply the rules in action.

Officiating Track & Field and Cross Country is a practical how-to guide that's been approved by the NFHS. This book is also the text for the *NFHS Officiating Track & Field and Cross Country Methods* online course, which has also been developed and produced by the American Sport Education Program (ASEP) and the NFHS. To find out how you can register for the online course, visit www.ASEP.com.

NFHS Officials Code of Ethics

Officials at an interscholastic athletic event are participants in the educational development of high school students. As such, they must exercise a high level of self-discipline, independence and responsibility. The purpose of this code is to establish guidelines for ethical standards of conduct for all interscholastic officials.

- Officials shall master both the rules of the game and the mechanics necessary to enforce the rules; they shall exercise authority in an impartial, firm and controlled manner.
- Officials shall work with each other and their state associations in a constructive and cooperative manner.
- Officials shall uphold the honor and dignity of the profession in all interaction with student-athletes, coaches, athletic directors, school administrators, colleagues and the public.
- Officials shall prepare themselves both physically and mentally, shall dress neatly and appropriately and shall comport themselves in a manner consistent with the high standards of the officiating profession.
- Officials shall be punctual and professional in the fulfillment of all contractual obligations.
- Officials shall remain mindful that their conduct influences the respect that student-athletes, coaches and the public hold for the profession.
- Officials shall, while enforcing the rules of play, remain aware of the inherent risk of injury that competition poses to student-athletes. When appropriate, they shall inform event management of conditions or situations that appear unreasonably hazardous.
- Officials shall take reasonable steps to educate themselves about recognizing emergency conditions that might arise during a competition.

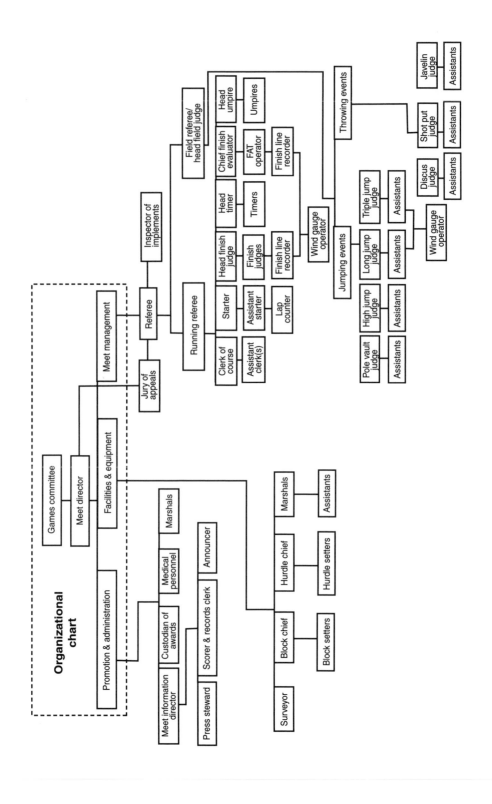

Organizational chart

- Games committee
- Meet director
  - Meet management
    - Jury of appeals
    - Referee
      - Inspector of implements
      - Field referee/head field judge
        - Chief finish evaluator
          - Head umpire
          - Umpires
        - FAT operator
        - Finish line recorder
        - Throwing events
          - Javelin judge
            - Assistants
          - Shot put judge
            - Assistants
          - Discus judge
            - Assistants
      - Running referee
        - Clerk of course
          - Assistant clerk(s)
        - Starter
          - Assistant starter
          - Lap counter
        - Head finish judge
          - Finish judges
          - Finish line recorder
        - Head timer
          - Timers
        - Wind gauge operator
        - Jumping events
          - Pole vault judge
            - Assistants
          - High jump judge
            - Assistants
          - Long jump judge
            - Assistants
          - Triple jump judge
            - Assistants
          - Wind gauge operator
  - Facilities & equipment
    - Surveyor
    - Block chief
      - Block setters
    - Hurdle chief
      - Hurdle setters
    - Marshals
      - Assistants
  - Promotion & administration
    - Meet information director
    - Press steward
    - Custodian of awards
    - Scorer & records clerk
    - Medical personnel
    - Announcer
    - Marshals

PART I

OFFICIATING BASICS

CHAPTER 1

Introduction to Officiating Track & Field and Cross Country

Maybe you remember October 18, 1968, when Bob Beamon broke—no, *shattered*—the world record in the long jump at the Mexico City Olympics. In an event in which records are usually broken by fractions of inches, Beamon broke the long-jump record by 21-¾ inches when he jumped 29 feet, 2-½ inches. Twenty-three years passed before another long-jumper finally topped Beamon's record, when Mike Powell jumped 29 feet, 4-½ inches, at the World Championships in 1991. Or maybe you recall Florence Griffith Joyner blazing down the Indianapolis track at the U.S. Olympic Trials on July 16, 1988, setting a world record of 10.49 in the 100 meters. More recently, many of us witnessed Michael Johnson blistering the Atlanta track on his way to a 200-meter world record of 19.32 in the 1996 Olympics.

These spectacular feats are among many highlights in the recent history of track and field and cross country. Such examples of electrifying individual achievement are part of what makes track and field and cross country so appealing to those of us who follow these sports and want to be a part of them. Track and field is among the world's oldest sports, with competitions dating back to the seventh century B.C. Known internationally as "athletics," track and field events are popular worldwide and are the centerpiece of the Summer Olympics. Track and field events are also extremely popular at the high school level. Well over 400,000 young women in the United States participate in track and field, making it the second most popular sport for high school girls. Nearly 500,000

young men take part in United States high school track and field events, a
participation rate that is topped only by football and basketball. Approximately 163,000 young women and 192,000 young men in United States
high schools are involved in cross country.

That's a lot of athletes trying to run faster, jump farther or higher and
throw farther than their competitors. It takes many knowledgeable officials to ensure all races, jumps and throws are executed in accordance with
the rules governing the events. Track and field is unique in that multiple
events take place simultaneously, requiring officials to know the rules of
several different events and respond to a variety of situations to ensure
that athletes have a fair and equal chance to compete.

Because of the relation of the two sports, you might enjoy officiating in
the fall at cross country meets and in the spring at track and field meets.
Whether you officiate one or both sports, we can help prepare you for
your role as an official by exploring the purpose and philosophy of officiating, discussing what it takes to get the job done and providing the tools,
techniques and mechanics you need to become a reliable and respected
official. We'll also describe the role of your state association and of the
National Federation of State High School Associations (NFHS) and the
educational support the federation offers high school officials.

Purpose and Philosophy

Your officiating philosophy is an important factor in your success
as an official. How you approach your duties, respond to challenging situations and continue to learn and apply your knowledge play
large roles in determining how much you enjoy being an official and
how good you are at it. As you gain experience, circumstances once
challenging for you become much easier; situations once problematic
become routine. You learn to anticipate problems and avoid pitfalls
and danger areas.

As an official, you have three essential purposes:

1. To ensure fair play by upholding the rules of the sport
2. To minimize risks for the athletes
3. To exercise authority in an impartial, firm and controlled manner

Ensuring Fair Play

At the foundation of all competition is fair play. Athletes, coaches and fans
expect the rules of a sport to be applied correctly and fairly. Competitors
want and deserve an "equal playing field," meaning, as an official, you
must know and apply the rules appropriately in all situations.

It's an official's responsibility to enforce the rules fairly and consistently.

To ensure fair competition, you must know the rules and how to enforce them fairly and consistently. When you do this, you're on your way toward being a good official.

In your role as an official, you should do all you can to help athletes compete legally, responsibly and fairly. Occasionally, some officials get the notion they're not doing their job unless they're disqualifying or penalizing athletes, as if they're traffic cops with ticket quotas to fill. This is far from the case. You're there to ensure the legality and fairness of the competition. Your purpose is to give the athletes the opportunity to compete fairly—not to overassert your authority and intrude on the activity.

Minimizing Risks

Like all sports, track and field and cross country have inherent risks of injury. Some injuries you can do nothing about—a sprinter pulls up, clutching his strained calf; a middle-distance runner is forced to sit out to heal her plantar fasciitis; two runners collide with each other. Who can forget Mary Decker Slaney tumbling to the infield in the 1984 Olympic

3,000 meters after her spikes caught Zola Budd's ankle? With the stress they put on their shoulders, arms, backs and knees, athletes in the throwing events are hardly immune to injury, either.

But many of the injuries that occur at meets are preventable. Many athletes and bystanders have been struck by a discus, shot or javelin, and some have been seriously injured. Athletes have been killed in pole-vaulting accidents; others have suffered permanent disabilities or serious injuries from landing, or bouncing, out of the pole-vault pit area. The NFHS does all it can to reduce the risk of injury. For example, the backs and sides of the discus circle are now fenced, and the pole-vault landing area has been enlarged and includes a common cover or pad extending over all sections of the pit. The hard, unyielding surfaces around the landing system are padded.

As an official, what can you do to prevent injuries? Here are four guidelines:

- Know and enforce the rules that minimize risk, including those regarding uniforms, venues and equipment use. The rules were written to minimize athletes' risks while allowing them to excel.

- Inspect the competition area before the meet begins, making sure the area is legal and safe. If it's not, ensure it is made so before allowing competition to begin.

- Maintain authority and control in all aspects, including giving clear signals to everyone present to stay clear of the area as athletes are warming up and competing.

- Know how to respond to injuries and emergency situations.

Exercising Authority

Exercise authority in an impartial, firm and controlled manner. You can know the rules backward and forward, but if you can't exercise the proper authority, you're going to have a difficult time as an official.

Everyone involved in, or with an interest in, the competition is looking to you to make the correct judgments and to do so in a manner that doesn't call extra attention to yourself but lets all concerned know that you know the rules, know how to apply them fairly and impartially and know how to take control in every situation. If you make indecisive calls or appear not to know the rules, you're headed for trouble. It's difficult to regain authority once you've lost it.

To gain and maintain authority, you must know the rules, be firm, decisive and consistent in your calls, retain control at all times and make every call impartial. When you do this you maintain your authority and uphold the honor and dignity of the profession. Coaches and athletes far prefer to have meets overseen by officials who know how to exercise their proper authority—because then they know what to expect. Just as athletes are expected to prepare themselves to do their best, officials are expected to exercise appropriate authority in conducting a meet. Even when you make a mistake—which will happen—never lose control of the situation.

Who Are Officials?

Track and field and cross country officials come from all walks of life, including teachers, bankers, insurance agents, business executives, factory workers and postal workers. Many, but by no means all, competed in track and field, cross country or both at the high school level or in college. Some are recently out of high school; others are nearing, or are into, retirement.

Despite their differences in age and life experience, good officials have much in common. Most of them are critical thinkers who can make decisions in the heat of the moment while maintaining calm and poise. They are able to act as peacekeepers and negotiators, and they know when to step into these roles. They know when and how to massage an ego without demeaning themselves or harming the integrity of the sport. They know when and how to sell a call. They have thick skins and an ample amount of patience.

The common denominator for all officials is their love for the sport. In many cases, officials are giving back to a sport that has given so much to them. Being an official is a great way to give back to a sport, to help a sport flourish, to play an integral role in the enjoyment of the sport by athletes, coaches and fans alike.

What Makes a Good Official?

Just as athletes need a mix of skills to excel, officials need a range of skills and competencies to be good officials. Sometimes these skills and competencies can seem almost contradictory.

For example, to be a good official, you have to "blend into the background" in one sense and yet be present and authoritative at the same time. You have to maintain control yet keep the meet focused on the athletes. In the highly emotional arena of sports, you must keep your head about you while all others are losing theirs. It's inevitable that you'll make a mistake now and then, so expect that to happen, but do your best to learn from your mistakes and strive never to repeat them.

Officiating is hard work. But there are many good officials out there, and they all got there through thorough preparation and dedication to

Officials must know the rules of the sport and execute them fairly and consistently.

their profession. You can join the ranks of good officials by following the nine prerequisites for good officiating described here:

1. Know the rules.

To be a competent official, study the rules thoroughly. In track and field, of course, you're not only judging how far a throw goes, how high or how long an athlete jumps or how fast an athlete runs—you're also judging whether the execution of the skill was legal. You can prepare yourself for making effective decisions of every nature by constantly reviewing the rules. When fundamentals become second nature and correct interpretations become routine, you know you have a firm grasp of the rules.

Of course, a big part of knowing the rules is knowing *exactly* which rules you're meant to follow. The technical rules for each event are generally the same nationwide, but administrative rules can differ from state to state. To stay on top of your state association adoptions, determine whom your state office has designated as the state rules interpreter. In addition, state associations have the authority to make decisions and interpret rulings in some areas. Again, consult your state association, which disseminates information for officials to ensure you're current with administrative rules and rule adoptions.

2. Know the mechanics.

Your knowledge of the rules might be great, but if your mechanics are poor, you'll have a hard time communicating your calls. For success, master the mechanics. Learn the proper positions for the different officials' roles, and practice them until positioning becomes second nature. Whether you're a novice or a veteran, look for opportunities to discuss and review position and coverage at clinics and to practice your mechanics.

3. Make calls positively and with good timing.

Be careful about rendering decisions prematurely. Make decisions positively and with good timing, but don't be hasty in raising your flag to indicate a foul. Call a foul when you're certain of the foul. Don't wait too long, though, because timidity or extended hesitation indicates a lack of confidence. Make all calls in a confident manner, which you'll develop with experience and practice.

Your positive and timely action goes far toward getting your call accepted. Cultivate your voice to increase your authority through your spoken word. A strong voice is a valuable asset. Make all calls loudly and clearly so you're heard by those you intend to hear you.

4. Ignore the fans.

Every crowd includes some fans who believe it's their duty to insult the officials. Totally ignore remarks from the fans. Those same fans who heckle you will lose respect for you if you react to their criticism or indicate you're aware of their heckling. And when this happens, their criticism becomes more intense. Two traits of good officials are to have a deaf ear toward fans and a thick skin impervious to barbs and catcalls.

5. Don't draw undue attention to yourself.

Don't be a showboat; execute your duties without flair. When you take care of your responsibilities with dignity and in conformance with accepted signals and procedures, you'll encourage athletes and spectators to accept your decisions. Being overly dramatic often accomplishes no good purpose, as such behavior frequently causes athletes to lose confidence in the decisions made by an "actor." Quiet dignity is more effective. Don't be self-important and bossy, but don't tolerate disrespect, either.

6. Be courteous to athletes and coaches, but don't fraternize with them.

Avoid visiting with athletes or coaches immediately before, during or after a meet. Never attempt to coach an athlete, and don't argue with athletes, coaches or team representatives; keep your discussions with these personnel brief and businesslike. A dignified attitude can often preclude and prevent an argument.

7. Hustle and be alert.

To be successful in officiating, stay on the alert and always keep an eye out. When you need to move, move briskly, and, as appropriate from time to time, urge athletes to hustle. Keep your head erect and maintain a posture and appearance of one who can properly discharge his or her responsibility.

8. Call them as you see them.

Your decision-making judgment sharpens with experience. Remember to base your decisions on fact. First, cover the situation according to proper procedures and mechanics. Second, and more important, rule on the situation exactly as you saw it. Yes, you'll make some mistakes from time to time, no matter how conscientious and efficient you are and regardless of your position and rules knowledge. When you make a mistake, you need not be unduly humbled or embarrassed. And never attempt to "even it up" after an error. Make each call on its own merits.

9. Maintain rapport and respect for other officials.

Have a mutual respect for your fellow officials. Friendliness and respect for them (and for the profession) contribute to confidence in one another. Support your fellow officials throughout the meet. When one official requests an opinion of another, the opinion should be given courteously to the official requesting it and be given to him or her only.

In addition to maintaining respect for other officials, do all you can to contribute to or maintain the great traditions of the sport. Give your chosen profession or avocation the best possible service. Carry out your assignments to the best of your ability, and maintain your integrity at all times.

Track and Field and Cross Country Official's Tools

Listed here are several tools you can use to excel as an official. The following are a few examples:

- *The current* NFHS Track and Field and Cross Country Rules Book. Get this book, learn it backward and forward and know it as well as you can possibly know it. Learn how to use this source for quick reference.
- NFHS Track and Field and Cross Country Case Book. Study the cases to strengthen your knowledge of how to rule in a wide variety of scenarios that can and do occur at meets.
- *Officiating resources.* Use this book as well as magazines, literature and other resources to help you hone your skills.
- *Firsthand experience.* Use every one of your officiating experiences to learn, improve and expand your knowledge of the sport and your ability to officiate.
- *Your fellow officials.* Learn from watching other good officials, either in person or on television. Watch their style, their mechanics, how they carry themselves, how they exercise their authority, how they make their calls and adapt to your own style.
- *Clinics and workshops.* Attend as many rules clinics as you can manage to make time for. If no clinics are offered in your area, suggest to some veteran local officials that they start a clinic of their own. And don't stop with one clinic or course—continue to learn throughout your career. Stay sharp, and never get complacent with your learning.
- *A journal.* Use a journal as a self-assessment tool, charting areas for improvement, successes, progress and things you learn from each assignment.
- *Review from others.* Request that a fellow official from your local chapter come watch you and critique your work.
- *Self-review.* Have a friend videotape your officiating at a meet for you to watch at a later time. You can often learn most by watching yourself.
- *Pre- and postmeet meetings.* These meetings are key learning times for officials, especially for beginners. If you're a new official, or even if you're a veteran, there's no shame in asking other officials for advice.

Officiating at the High School Level

Officiating track and field and cross country at the high school level is in many ways similar to officiating at other levels, but there are some aspects that make the high school experience unique.

You might have officiated at youth levels where the officials sometimes "coach" the athletes during a meet, giving them technique tips or allowing them to bend the rules as they learn the event. This doesn't happen at the high school level; you neither bend the rules nor coach the athletes. You simply call the event fairly and authoritatively.

Sometimes it can be hard on track and field officials to refrain from offering technique suggestions to athletes, because there's a certain amount of down time when an athlete is near an official, and quite often the athlete's coach is not nearby. It's tempting to shift into offering some suggestions—but don't cross this line. You can't assist athletes in any way. Imagine if you were a coach and you saw an official giving a rival athlete some help. You wouldn't see this as fair or professional.

When you officiate at the high school level, you'll likely work various types of meets, including duals, triangulars and invitationals, that lead up to state qualifying meets and the state meet itself. The main difference in officiating at the bigger meets is in the number of officials involved and the amount of administration required. We'll take a closer look at this when we get into officials' responsibilities in the next chapter.

As a high school track and field or cross country official, you're encouraged to become part of the NFHS Officials Association. Through your state officials' association, you can receive assignments, attend annual rules meetings to learn new rules and hone your techniques and other skills and attend clinics throughout the year. Take advantage of your membership within both the NFHS Officials Association and your state organization to continue to develop your skills as an official.

Also be aware that state interpreters from across the country meet annually to discuss the application of NFHS rules. From these meetings, interpretations are published and distributed to all state associations. The *Officials' Quarterly* also provides interpretations to members.

In this chapter we've focused on the foundational elements of being a track and field or cross country official. We've discussed the purpose and philosophy of officiating; who officials are and what makes them effective; officials' tools; and officiating at the high school level. In the next chapter you'll learn about your responsibilities at a meet and the procedures in place to carry out those responsibilities.

CHAPTER 2

MEET PROCEDURES AND RESPONSIBILITIES

Because track and field involves many athletes competing in a variety of events, with multiple events taking place simultaneously, a significant number of officials are required who know their duties and responsibilities and whose efforts are well coordinated by a games committee and meet director. Administering cross country meets, while simpler in nature, likewise requires careful planning, knowledge and expertise in handling the duties that allow the event to move along efficiently.

In the first part of this chapter, we'll take a look at the ins and outs of administering a track and field meet, including who's involved and what the basic responsibilities are. Following that, we'll take a similar look at cross country.

Track and Field Procedures and Responsibilities

The responsibilities of administering a track and field meet rest on the shoulders of members of the games committee, the meet director and the meet officials. In the following sections we'll discuss the basic responsibilities of the people in these roles.

The Games Committee

The games committee is responsible for conducting a track and field meet. In dual meets, this committee might consist solely of a meet director or a referee; in invitational meets, the committee usually consists of several additional people. At the state qualifying and state meets, the state association appoints a games committee.

Regardless of which or how many officials make up the games committee, this committee is responsible for the general supervision of the meet, which includes securing sanctioning for the meet from the proper authority. The games committee also serves the following functions:

- Arranges for competition areas and necessary equipment for the meet
- Invites schools to participate
- Establishes reasonable entry deadlines
- Secures appropriate meet officials
- Provides a registration area to distribute meet packets
- Arranges a location in which coaches make their final declaration of entries (for states that allow scratches)

Meet administration can be categorized into three areas: promotion and administration, facilities and equipment and meet management. We'll address the first two areas in this chapter and discuss meet-management issues in chapters 3 and 4.

In addition to determining which schools are involved, when and where the meet will be held and who will officiate at the meet, the games committee is responsible for many other decisions, including

- the number of heats required for an event,
- the heat lanes and assignments,
- the assignments of athletes to flights for preliminary competitions,
- the number of athletes and the criteria to qualify for the next round of competition,
- the method of baton exchange in relays not run in lanes,
- the starting height and successive heights of the crossbar,
- the throwing area locations,
- the order in which athletes take their trials,
- the time limit or number of warm-up opportunities for athletes in the field events and
- the time limit and procedure for excusing an athlete to take part in another event.

The games committee's duties also include determining the details and specifics of a meet to ensure the meet is conducted smoothly and fairly. This jurisdiction can be categorized into three areas: *general*, pertaining to all athletes or to overall meet supervision; *track*, pertaining to running events; and *field*, pertaining to field events.

Principles of Heat Drawing

When a competition requires multiple heats, procedures are in place to guide the games committee in drawing up the heats and placing the runners in them. Though heat drawing is now usually done with the aid of computer software, here are the proper procedures to follow. When times are available for all qualified contestants, form heats in accordance with the following guidelines:

1. Weigh *place* first.
2. Weigh *time* second.
3. Working from left to right and right to left, group and seed first-place winners by their times, group and seed second-place winners by their times, group and seed third-place winners by their times and group and seed fourth-place winners by their times. You will group and seed athletes as follows:
   - 1a = fastest first-place contestant from all the heats
   - 2a = fastest second-place contestant from all the heats
   - 1b = second-fastest first-place contestant from all the heats (and so on)
4. In the first round of competition only, if two athletes from the same team are in the same heat, move the athlete with the slower time to another heat by switching him or her with an athlete of the nearest comparable place and time. Make this comparison by weighing place first and time second. (Again, not necessary if the race is seeded by computer.)
5. If all heats don't have an equal number of contestants, draw for the extra contestant assignment to heat by lot (random selection). For example, when an odd number of runners have qualified for two heats, the runner with the lowest place and the slowest time is placed by drawing lots in one of the heats.

The games committee then decides which are the preferred lanes, based on the event and track conditions, and assigns lanes with priority given to the best qualifiers.

When setting up heats based solely on qualifying times, rank competitors according to their times, taking into consideration the number of preliminary heats. For example, in seeding runners into six heats based on qualifying times, seed them as shown here:

(continued)

Principles of Heat Drawing (continued)

Heat 1	Heat 2	Heat 3	Heat 4	Heat 5	Heat 6
1	2	3	4	5	6
12	11	10	9	8	7
13	14	15	16	17	18

The numbers refer to the seeds (or rankings), with the runner with the top time being given the number 1 seed, and so on. Continue in this manner, placing the runners, based on their times, from left to right (as with runners 1 to 6, as shown) and from right to left (as with runners 7 to 12) until all runners have been seeded.

General Responsibilities

General responsibilities of the games committee involve uniform and equipment regulations; determining the extent of its own jurisdiction and informing all involved in the meet of this information; and the procedural duties of administering a track and field meet. Among the general responsibilities are

- determining the length of spikes allowed on all-weather surfaces;
- specifying the marking material, if any, and the number and location of checkmarks allowed on the track, runway or approach apron;
- providing batons, starting blocks and throwing-event implements;
- determining and marking restricted areas in which only competitors and meet officials are allowed;
- declaring that the jersey must be tucked into the shorts;
- defining the area of competition in which removal of any portion of the team uniform, except shoes, is prohibited;
- being the jury of appeals or appointing a jury of appeals (the referee can't be a member of the jury);
- appointing separate or assistant referees, as deemed necessary;
- changing the announced order of events, the number of heats and the number to qualify, if necessary;
- restricting the wearing of costumes, hats, baseball caps, kerchiefs, bandanas, unapproved sunglasses, jewelry and so on that aren't part of the traditional school uniform;

Officials must enforce regulations determined by the games committee, including the legality of uniforms.

- restricting the use of electronic devices, such as cell phones; and
- specifying a time within 48 hours of the conclusion of the meet for the correction of scoring errors.

Track Responsibilities

The games committee also has duties to fulfill specific to the track portion of a track and field meet. These responsibilities focus on finish-line procedures and how to respond when a timing device malfunctions. Track responsibilities for the games committee include the following:

- Approving the use of an amplifier system for starting running events
- Determining the procedure for handling a lapped runner
- Authorizing official pictures of the finish to assist in the final decision of places
- Designating a procedure to follow in case the fully automatic timing (FAT) system malfunctions

Field Responsibilities

Finally, the games committee has several responsibilities related to the field events. These duties are in place to ensure that the events are fairly contested, that participants understand the parameters of their events and that the events are conducted safely. Field responsibilities for the games committee include the following:

- Placing markers to the side of the landing pit to mark records or minimum qualifying standards
- Determining when field events will be finished
- Specifying the number of throws and distances to be measured in the throwing events
- Specifying the number of jumps and distances to be measured in the horizontal events
- Designating an area for pole-vault coaches
- Designating the use of 34.92 or 40-degree throwing sectors in the shot and discus throw
- Determining the procedure for impounding and releasing illegal implements

Meet Director

As mentioned, the meet director is sometimes the only member of the games "committee"; this is particularly common in dual meets. In such a case, the meet director is charged with fulfilling all duties that help the meet run smoothly.

On top of any or all duties required as a member of the games committee, the meet director also supervises the conduct of the meet. Usually, when entry limitations at a meet are more restrictive than NFHS rules, the meet director shall announce the number of contestants who may represent a school and the number of events in which they may compete. The meet director determines the regulations using the standards listed in the rules book. Generally speaking, a meet director has nine major areas of responsibility for a meet, as described here.

1. Secure a proper meet sanction.

If a sanction is required by the state association or the NFHS, the meet director obtains a meet sanction at least 30 days prior to the meet. The state association should be contacted to determine the proper sanctioning procedure.

2. Reserve the site.

This is typically routine, as the site is generally the home facility. However, a hosting school sometimes uses another site, and it's the meet director's responsibility to ensure the site is reserved. The necessary contracts to ensure the facility is available on the desired date should be read carefully before being signed.

3. Send invitations and entry forms.

The meet director sends invitations to all schools to be included in the competition. Depending on the size and type of meet, most or all of the meet information should be included in the invitation. See "Meet Information Checklist" on page 124 in appendix A for a listing of this information.

4. Send invitations to meet officials.

The number of officials needed per event ranges from three officials and two workers at a very small meet to five officials and several workers per field event at larger meets. A self-addressed postcard should be included with the invitation so the official can indicate whether he or she accepts or refuses the assignment. Include the assignment date, kind of competition, directions to the site (including a map of the competition area and other pertinent information about the venue) and the official's personal schedule, which describes where and when the official is scheduled to work, information about meals and parking and health and safety reminders relating to sunscreen or water provisions. Other information to send along with the invitation includes any current interpretations by the NFHS and reviews of rule changes and tie-breaking procedures. Finally, the invitation should include the date, time and location of any training sessions or premeet officials' meetings; information defining required dress for meet officials; and, when appropriate, a contract to be signed and returned.

5. Oversee the publicity and program committee.

This area of responsibility involves promoting the meet, the printed program and media relations. For promotion, the meet director provides the pertinent details of the meet, news media to be contacted and a diagram of the facilities, including the dressing area, restrooms and restricted areas. For the printed program, the following information is generally included: the schedule of events and competition times; records (and perhaps pictures of past and returning champions); flight, heat and lane assignments; advancement procedure for competitors from preliminaries to finals; the team and individual scoring system to be used; the number of allowed entrants and participation limits; awards; and advertising. Media relations involve defining and distributing policies on interviews, producing and posting posters and photos, and establishing procedures for releasing meet results to the media.

6. Oversee the registration committee.

The meet director oversees the registration procedures, which, in most cases, are performed by a committee. The registration process should be clear and simple for all coaches and athletes to follow. At registration,

Meet Aids

Athletes, officials and spectators can be aided at a track and field meet in many ways. These aids can improve safety for athletes, improve communication among officials and improve the enjoyment of the sport for the fans. Read on to see how each group of meet participants can be assisted, thus making for a safer, well-run, more enjoyable meet.

Athlete Aids

A medical professional and a trainer should be on site for all meets. In addition, meet directors should consider the following items as standard necessities for athletes for all meets:

- A clearly marked, accessible first aid tent
- Clerking area protected from weather by a tent or canopy
- Chairs or benches for athletes at various events
- Scooters, carts or baskets to transport athletes' warm-ups from the starting line to the finish area
- Water stations

Officiating Aids

Items on the following list, though not required, are common aids for meet officials:

- A wireless communication system
- Fully automatic timing (FAT)
- A centrally located headquarters tent so that event judges have easy access to the referee, meet director and field referee
- Distinctive pieces of clothing such as caps, shirts, jackets or vests to distinguish one official from another
- Printing timer (used to record individual times in longer track races)

Spectator Aids

Items on the following list, though not all required, are good to have on hand to enhance the experience of the spectators:

- A scoreboard (lighted, if possible) on which entries, results and brief messages can be displayed
- Rotating sign boards for field events on which competitors' numbers and performances are manually placed

(continued)

Meet Aids (continued)

- Crossbar height indicators
- Long-jump and triple-jump distance indicators
- Distance indicators for arc lines in the throwing events
- Lane numbers for sprints and hurdles
- Red flags to indicate fouls and white flags to indicate legal trials in the throwing and jumping events
- Yellow flags to indicate potential violations and white flags to indicate "all clear" in running events
- Markers to indicate current records in the field events
- Time indicator showing the running (ongoing) time for the event, such as a Chronomix display

coaches get their team packets, which include contestant numbers and pins, instruction sheets, an appeals form, relay forms and any other necessary forms. A table should be designated for entry changes and special messages to coaches and athletes so that coaches can report scratches in events. Bulletin boards, with schedules and other important information clearly posted, should be placed in areas accessible to coaches and athletes.

7. Ensure proper equipment is available.

Another duty of the meet director is to ensure the equipment necessary to run the meet is on hand and ready for use. See "Event Equipment Checklist" in appendix A on page 125 for equipment lists for track and field meets.

8. Oversee premeet assignments.

Premeet assignments include preparing the track and field areas for competition (e.g., setting performance indicators and visible timing devices in place; checking all lines, marks and zones to ensure they're properly marked; and checking all equipment to be used). Other assignments are putting supplies into officials' packets, confirming the premeet meeting time and location for all officials and determining how to document the flow of results.

9. Oversee postmeet assignments.

When the meet is finished, the meet director has duties still remaining. Postmeet tasks include cleanup of the site; returning equipment and supplies to the proper places; distributing results to schools and the media and placing information on appropriate Web sites; and sending out thank-you letters to all workers and officials, including both paid members and volunteers. Finally, the meet director evaluates how the meet was conducted, noting shortcomings and mistakes so that they can be improved on in the next meet.

Meet Officials

As you know, many officials are needed to conduct a track and field meet, especially for invitational meets. Here's a list of typical meet officials:

Overall Meet Administration
- Referee
- A jury of appeals (not including the referee)
- Inspector of implements

Running Events Administration
- Running referee
- Clerk and assistant clerks
- Starter, assistant starters and lap counters
- Head finish judge, finish judges and finish-line recorders
- Head timer and timers
- Chief finish evaluator, FAT operator and wind gauge operator
- Head umpire and umpires

Field Events Administration
- Head field judge or field referee
- Pole-vault judge and assistants
- High-jump judge and assistants
- Long-jump judge and assistants
- Triple-jump judge and assistants
- Wind gauge operator
- Discus judge and assistants
- Shot-put judge and assistants
- Javelin judge and assistants

The duties of most of these officials, including the inspector of implements, are detailed in chapters 3 and 4. Here we'll look at the duties of two types of officials who govern the overall meet: the referee and the jury of appeals.

Referee

The referee is in charge of all activities during a competition and supervises all meet officials. The referee has the sole authority to rule on infractions or irregularities not covered within the rules, though the referee may seek the advice of the assistant referee, head umpire or field referee before making a ruling. The referee also answers questions not specifically under the jurisdiction of other officials.

Responsibilities of the referee can be categorized into premeet responsibilities and responsibilities during the meet.

Premeet Responsibilities

We all know the referee has many duties to carry out during a meet, but he or she also has responsibilities before a meet. By attending to these responsibilities, the referee can often avert many problems or communication gaffes that might otherwise occur. In taking care of business before the meet, the referee is setting the stage for a safe, smooth and efficient meet to take place. The three main premeet responsibilities of a referee are obtaining and reviewing all games committee information, meeting with other officials and communicating with coaches and team captains.

1. Obtain and review all games committee information.

The games committee, appointed by the committee or host, typically includes the head coach from each participating school team. Information provided to the games committee explains the duties of the committee, when and where the committee will confer prior to the meet and any postmeet requirements, such as certifying qualifiers for the next level of competition. The games committee is also responsible for all competition areas and event equipment. For instance, for the pole vault, the committee should ensure the landing system, planting box, upright standards positioning and all surfaces meet proper standards.

2. Meet with other officials.

The referee should meet with the meet director, running and field referee(s), clerk(s) of the course, head finish judge and head umpire. During this meeting, areas of responsibilities during the meet are defined and clarified.

3. Communicate with coaches and team captains.

The referee must communicate with coaches and team captains, either verbally or in writing, to address proper sporting behavior, to certify that all athletes are properly equipped and uniformed and to discuss any special circumstances, procedures and information pertaining to the meet.

A few examples of topics the referee should address with coaches and team captains include when boys and girls are going to compete together in an event but be scored separately (such a decision would need unanimous agreement among coaches), events that would not be contested for a particular meet (again, this decision requires unanimous agreement among coaches), which track markings are allowed and which areas are restricted. Other topics might include state association adoptions (if any), entry limits, starting height in vertical jumps, number of attempts in the throws and the horizontal jumps, and other issues depending on the circumstances.

Meet Responsibilities

Of course the referee's main duty during a meet is to ensure fair competition, which requires thorough knowledge of the rules, an ability to supervise officials, good communication skills and enough wisdom to apply the rules fairly.

The referee is a bit like an orchestra conductor, directing, in this case, the flow of events; overseeing that everything is running smoothly and fairly; and guiding the performance of the other officials. All officials must be knowledgeable and able to respond to any situation that might occur during their events; the referee should ensure each member of the officiating team is up to the task. Usually, the knowledge and wisdom required to take on all this responsibility comes through experience. An extremely knowledgeable and competent referee is an invaluable asset to a track and field meet.

A referee's authority begins on arrival at the meet site and concludes 30 minutes after the last event's results have been announced or made official. Except for any appeals procedure established before the meet, the referee has the power to make all final decisions. The referee shall collaborate with the games committee when an emergency situation, such as hazardous weather, requires suspension of the meet.

If the referee observes an infraction committed by a runner, and the infraction isn't noted by an umpire or other official, the referee may disqualify the runner. When a competitor is to be warned or disqualified, the referee personally notifies the athlete or the athlete's coach.

The referee checks and certifies record performances in all events. In addition, the referee must approve the official scorer's final results, sign the scorebook and record the time the meet was officially concluded.

Jury of Appeals

Sometimes the games committee appoints a jury of appeals for a meet. In such a case, the jury, which consists of an odd number of people (typically three, five or seven), serves as the final board of appeals. In many cases, the games committee serves as the jury of appeals. The jury doesn't automatically convene but does so on an as-needed basis. The jury rules in cases in which a coach who is protesting a ruling to the referee is not satisfied with the referee's judgment. If after talking to the referee, the coach still feels that the terms and conditions of competition or the application of the rules have been misapplied or misinterpreted by the referee or other official, he or she can make a written appeal to the jury (see "Track and Field and Cross Country Appeal Form" in appendix A on page 126). The jury remains available until 30 minutes after the final event.

If coaches believe that rules have been misapplied, they must file an appeal within 30 minutes of the announcement of the event results. Correction of clerical or team scoring errors may be corrected up to 48 hours after the end of the meet, unless another time period has been specified in advance by the games committee or meet director. Corrections of meet results involving ineligible participants don't fall within the 48-hour limit and may be made at any time.

Coaches can file a protest for failure to follow a procedure contained in the terms and conditions of competition as announced in advance by the meet director or games committee. Such a protest might include items such as the time schedule, number of qualifiers to advance, number of trials or other concerns.

Coaches may *not* appeal these situations:

- Any judgment decision pertaining to violations or alleged violations of the rules
- A decision made by the finish judges or timers that doesn't involve misapplication of a rule or the terms and conditions of competition
- Whether a start is fair and legal

Meet Promotion and Administration

The promotion and administration of a meet is integral to the meet being successfully conducted. The many tasks involved in promoting and administering a meet are divided among these people or groups:

- Information director
- Press steward
- Meet announcer
- Meet scorer
- Records clerk
- Custodian of awards
- Medical personnel

Information Director

The information director is in charge of getting the right information at the right time to the right people. The individual in this role distributes premeet publicity releases to all appropriate news media, distributes press credentials and establishes policies for photographers in the infield, field events and starting and finish-line areas. He or she also designates press box seating assignments and establishes policies for interviewing coaches and competitors. Meet program layout, contents and advertising also fall under the information director's duties, as does the handling of other promotional projects, such as buttons, caps, T-shirts and the like.

Press Steward

The press steward and information director might be the same person. The press steward manages the press box area and serves as the liaison among the media and the competitors, coaches and officials. The press steward also provides a list of entries for each event, including the full name, number and team for each athlete and the event record. The steward also provides the running order of relay team members and the full name and school affiliation of each coach.

The press steward is responsible for distributing results following the completion of each event. (We should note that sometimes the meet scorer takes on this task; the meet director should clarify who has this responsibility before the event starts.) In dealing with the media, the steward uses discretion and good judgment while conveying the best interests of competitors and meet administration. Finally, the press steward distributes final results and identifies record performances.

Meet Announcer

A knowledgeable public-address announcer helps create and maintain spectator interest in the meet. The announcer's primary job involves helping keep the meet on schedule, aiding competitors in reporting on time, alerting coaches of upcoming events and keeping spectators informed.

It's prudent for an announcer to prepare a script, including an opening and closing statement, and to be familiar with qualifying procedures for each event and with scoring procedures. In addition, a good announcer learns the proper pronunciation of entrants' names, speaks clearly and slowly and is serious and courteous while calling out events. Note that the first call for an event should be 15 minutes before the event is to begin; the second call should occur 10 minutes before the event; and the final call should be 5 minutes before the event. When making the first call for a field event, the announcer should identify the location of the event. For track events, the announcer should identify the location of the starting line for the first event and the new location if it changes.Figure 2.1 is a sample beginning of an announcer's time schedule. An announcer should fill out such a schedule for the entire meet, using this sample as a guide, adjusting only as necessary for schedule changes.

The announcer should use the same procedure as identified above to introduce all competitors, including noting lane number, athlete's number and full name, and athlete's school. Athletes should step forward in their lanes as they're introduced. Other information announced at this time is the record for the event, including the name of the record holder, the school and the year the record was established.

The announcer is silent during the starter's commands and maintains that silence when the starting device is up. After a race, the announcer announces results and coordinates the awards presentation.

Other duties for the announcer include keeping spectators informed of events they might have missed (this particularly applies to field events), periodically announcing team points, adjusting the time schedule if the meet gets behind schedule and announcing the location of medical services, restrooms, concessions, the lost and found station and so on.

4:00	First call 3,200-meter relay
4:05	Second call 3,200-meter relay
4:10	Last call 3,200-meter relay
4:11	Welcome to all spectators, coaches, participants; review placing and scoring
4:13	Play national anthem
4:14	Announce entries for 110-meter high hurdles, record holder, etc.
4:15	3,200-meter relay
	First call 100-meter high hurdles
4:20	Second call 100-meter high hurdles
4:25	Last call 100-meter high hurdles
	First call 100-meter dash
	Announce results of 3,200-meter relay
4:29	Lane assignments, etc.; 100-meter high hurdles
4:30	100-meter high hurdles
	Second call 100-meter dash
4:35	Last call 100-meter dash
4:40	100-meter dash

FIGURE 2.1   Sample announcer's time schedule.

The best announcers have a good knowledge of the rules and officiating mechanics and make announcements only when necessary. Announcers shouldn't talk just to fill the silence.

Meet Scorer

Track and field requires accurate and prompt recording of the results from each event at its completion. The scorer and scoring assistant should position in an area that allows immediate access to the results of each event; together, the two keep a record of the competitors, the point winners in each event and the team scores. The scorer delivers these results to the meet director and referee at the end of the meet.

The scorer or press steward is responsible for immediate distribution of all results to media and coaches. (The meet director should clarify which person is responsible for this task before the event.) The scorer should compile result summaries as the meet progresses and make copies of the complete meet results available as soon as possible after the meet ends.

Scorers use a score sheet for each event (see "Team Score Sheet" in appendix A on page 127), the size of which depends on the number of teams in the meet.

Scorers should immediately resolve any scoring irregularities; they shouldn't wait until the end of the meet. A slight delay during the meet is far preferable to an error detected after the meet.

It's a good idea for the scorer to list the top five or six teams going into the last event and be ready to finalize the results quickly after the event ends. The scorer then distributes the final team results without delay so officials can present team trophies while participants and spectators are still present.

The scorer delivers all meet records to the referee for signature and time certification at the end of the meet, and then to the meet director. The scorer is usually required to sign the application forms requesting verification of record performances. The scorer ensures all team totals and records are complete and accurate.

Records Clerk

The records clerk is in charge of all clerical work involving meet records. This individual should have a form (provided by the meet director) listing all track and all field events plus a complete list of the full name, number, school affiliation and city for each athlete entered.

If a national record is tied or broken, the records clerk completes the required number of copies of the record application form, which entails filling out all the requested information (e.g., name, school, time, height, distance and anemometer reading, date) and circulating the form to the proper officials for signatures. The proper officials include the head event officials, referees and the wind gauge operator for sprints and field event judges for jumps and throws. Applications for records must also have the signature of the high school principal, the captain of the relay team and a representative of the state association office. It's best to secure as many of the required signatures as possible before the meet concludes because obtaining signatures through the mail can take a long time.

The records clerk submits the meet record applications to the referee or meet director at the end of the meet. Copies of the NFHS record application are available through the state association office (see "High School Track and Field Record Application" in appendix A on page 128).

Custodian of Awards

The custodian of awards must carefully inventory and arrange all awards before the meet starts. Place the awards stand in an area convenient to award winners and visible to spectators.

Make the awards ceremony as impressive as possible. Athletes should wear only their regular school uniform as they appear on the stand. Some personal (but brief) comments to the winner by the presenter are appropriate. The awards can be presented immediately following a completed event by escorting the place-winners directly to the awards stand, or the awards ceremony can be delayed by one event. The delayed method allows athletes to gain their composure before stepping onto the stand. Either way, it's best to have an awards plan in place prior to the meet.

The announcer and custodian of awards work closely to coordinate the awards ceremonies. The results of each event are delivered (typically by students) to the awards stand as soon as possible. An awards steward escorts the place-winners to the stand. As their names, schools, places and distances or times are announced, the presenter gives them their award. In case of ties, the custodian of awards should have the tied competitors flip a coin or draw lots to determine who gets the award. If a duplicate award will be provided later, the custodian of awards should record the name and address as well as the event and place won so the award can be mailed. The custodian of awards provides this information to the meet director at the end of the meet.

In small meets, it might be appropriate to put awards for each team in envelopes and have the coach pick up the envelope at the end of the meet. The custodian should mark on the envelope the various events and places won and have the coach double-check and certify the receipt of the awards.

Medical Personnel

Medical personnel should be present for the entire meet, which includes the availability of an approved medical professional as well as a first aid center. This center should be staffed by medical personnel such as a registered nurse, a certified trainer or an EMT. An ambulance service should be available, and the local hospital should know about the event. The meet director should outline all related medical information in the invitation packet sent to schools participating in the meet.

The meet director informs the approved medical professional about the specific location of all medical personnel and the first aid station. Medical personnel should examine any competitor whose physical ability to complete his or her competition is doubtful. The personnel should provide a written certificate to the referee following any medical examination. The meet physician's decision on whether the athlete can compete is final.

Don't permit a competitor who has been rendered apparently unconscious during a meet to resume participation in that meet without written authorization from a medical professional.

A competitor who is bleeding or has an open wound or an excessive amount of blood on his or her uniform may complete the running event or field event trial; however, the competitor may not participate further until appropriate treatment has been administered and the uniform has been cleaned up or changed.

Meet Facilities and Equipment

No meet is successfully conducted without knowledgeable officials ensuring that the facilities and equipment are legal, safe and ready for competition. The officials in charge of facilities and equipment are listed here:

- Surveyor
- Block chief and block setters
- Hurdle chief and hurdle setters
- Marshal and assistant marshals

Note that the inspector of implements and the referee have responsibilities and jurisdiction here as well. For example, if the referee notes an unsafe facility, he or she can judge that an event cannot be conducted unless the facility is made safe for competition. Likewise, an inspector of implements, in carrying out his or her duties, can deem certain equipment illegal. The referee's duties are described earlier in this chapter; the inspector of implement's duties are covered in chapter 4.

The officials just listed are the "behind-the-scenes" officials who carry out much of the grunt work. In performing these tasks they ensure safety and fairness in competition. In the following sections we'll take a look at these officials' duties.

If the legality or safety of equipment or an area is in question, the referee may make a call on such.

Surveyor

The surveyor inspects and measures the track and all takeoffs and landing pits for the jumps and vaults, the throwing circles for the shot and discus, the foul lines for the javelin and the exchange zones for the relays. The surveyor also determines whether the course is level and presents a written statement of these findings to the games committee and the referee. After a track has been altered or striped, it usually needs to be recertified.

Block Chief and Block Setters

The block chief is responsible for supplying starting blocks prior to the start of each race that requires them. In addition to furnishing the blocks, the block chief often assists athletes by providing instructions on how to set the blocks. The block chief has a crew of 8 to 10 student workers who help place the blocks in each lane and remove them immediately after each start. In some situations, block setters may be asked to apply weight or pressure to a starting block to help stabilize it during the start of a race.

Hurdle Chief and Hurdle Setters

The hurdle chief is usually assisted by 10 to 20 hurdle setters and sets the flight nearest the starting line first so hurdlers can practice starts while remaining hurdles are being set. Hurdle setters must take care to set each flight of hurdles at the proper height and at the prescribed point in each lane. (Hurdle heights are 30 and 33 inches for girls' low and high hurdles and 36 and 39 inches for boys' intermediate and high hurdles.) Hurdle setters must also adjust the hurdle weights properly.

The hurdle chief notifies the head umpire when all the hurdles have been properly set. It's the hurdle chief's duty to reset hurdles and check alignment after each heat and to remove hurdles from the track as soon as the event is completed.

Marshal and Assistant Marshals

The head marshal should use a diagram from the meet director that shows where each assistant marshal is to be positioned. The marshals keep all restricted areas free from unauthorized personnel at all times. Other meet officials working in these areas should assist the marshals in this task. Give particular attention to landing areas in the throwing events, jump and vault runways, and starting and finishing areas. Don't permit coaches on the track or infield area. (Exception: Pole-vault coaches may be in the assigned pole-vault coaching area, which could be on the infield.) Instead, provide them a reserved section in the stands. Photographers and other media must remain in their assigned areas as well. They should not be allowed into areas that will block spectators' view or interfere with meet personnel.

Restricted areas should be well marked and corded off with ropes or flags. All athletes, coaches, meet personnel and the media should be alerted to what areas are restricted. Figure 2.2 is an example of a restricted area around the finish line.

In figure 2.2, the relay restriction line is designated by a broken line. Runners must remain in this area until instructed to move onto the track. After passing the baton, a runner should stand still or jog straight ahead and wait to step off the track until it's clear.

Instruct runners to warm up away from the starting and finish lines, and gather runners in upcoming heats or races away from the starting line.

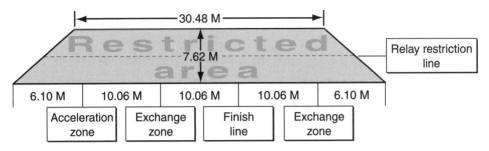

FIGURE 2.2   Restricted areas.

In field events, restricted areas include all runways and throwing areas. These areas must be kept completely clear of everyone except athletes competing in the events being conducted in those areas.

Cross Country Procedures and Responsibilities

The meet director should prepare a list of assignments to be completed before the meet. These assignments should be arranged in chronological order according to the date they need to be completed. Meet directors should delegate some of the work but must be prepared to handle all matters under their jurisdiction. Following are many of the typical assignments of meet directors:

- Arrange for the site
- Obtain proper sanctioning as required
- Prepare and mail instruction sheets to each coach and official
- Prepare advance publicity
- Select and assign officials
- Identify restricted areas
- Prepare signs, flags or course markers and finish chute
- Prepare checker sheets and numbers for each contestant
- Obtain safety pins for numbers
- Check entries of each team
- Secure accessible restroom facilities
- Arrange for medical services
- Prepare a time schedule (coaches' meeting, officials' meeting, anthem, team introductions and races)
- Award trophies and medals

- Report results to the area media and place on appropriate Web sites
- Mail meet summaries to each participating school
- Arrange plans for inclement weather
- Arrange video camera provisions for the race finish
- Obtain a tape recorder to use as a backup to cross-check numbers worn by the finishing competitors
- Provide finish tickets, computer barcodes or computer chips

The meet director should do an inventory of the required workers and then secure the people needed. When requested, participating schools will often assist in providing workers.

Once the officials and meet workers are in place, they should become thoroughly familiar with their duties and responsibilities. Instruction sheets prepared in advance should assist with this task (see "Cross Country Team Instruction Sheet" in appendix A on page 131). The meet director should also send a team instruction sheet to coaches of all participating schools at least five days before the meet.

The following list indicates the type and number of officials we recommend on the course for a meet (note that if computer chips are used to record finishes, no chute is necessary, and the checkers, caller, chute umpires and timers are not needed):

- *Meet director:* 1
- *Referee or starter:* 1
- *Chute director:* 1
- *Checkers:* 3
- *Caller:* 1
- *Finish-line judges:* 2
- *Clerk of the course:* 1
- *Chute umpires:* 4
- *Course umpires:* 4 to 6
- *Marshals:* as needed on every turn, blind spot, mile mark, terrain change or hazard
- *Timers:* 3

The meet director should have all officials and meet workers wear common attire—a cap, jacket, arm band or vest, for instance—that identifies them as meet officials.

In the sections that follow are brief descriptions of the duties of cross country officials.

The Referee, Starter and Clerk of the Course

Although the referee, starter and clerk of the course have distinct duties, in reality the same individual often carries out the duties of all three officials.

- *Referee.* To help ensure fairness of competition and adherence to the rules of conduct, the referee disqualifies any participant for unsporting behavior or for any violation of the rules governing the competition.

- *Starter.* The starter starts the race. The no-false start rule is in effect for cross country. (For more on starting the race, see chapter 5.)
- *Clerk of the course.* The clerk of the course places the teams in proper position on the starting line. Meet management might have already conducted a drawing by lot; in this case, coaches would have received their team's starting line assignments in the premeet information.

The clerk instructs the runners before the start of the race, explaining the commands and the recall procedures. The clerk should also check and enforce uniform, jewelry, visible apparel and shoe regulations. Finally, the clerk ensures that chips (when used) are properly placed.

Marshals

Cross country marshals ensure only the proper personnel are in the competitive area as a meet is taking place. Specifically, marshals are authorized to keep the competitive area free of all individuals except officials, runners and others authorized by the games committee. This is necessary for the safety of the athletes, who risk injury if unauthorized personnel move into their path. Restricting the competitive area also cuts down on confusion as officials try to account for all participating runners.

Course Umpires

Course umpires have one main duty: to report infractions to the referee. Thus, umpires are placed at points along the course where infractions are most likely to occur, such as at turns, where a runner might cut the turn.

Umpires help ensure that races are run fairly, that a runner doesn't gain an unfair advantage by cutting a course or by impeding or fouling another runner. Course umpires report rule violations to the referee.

Timers

The timers record the called-out times of all competitors who finish the race. A printing timer can be used to time each finisher. Timers can also be assigned to designated positions along the course to call out elapsed time to runners during the race.

Note that timers are not needed when computer chips are used, though split timers should still be used to call out elapsed time during the race.

Finish-Line Judges

Finish-line judges stand outside the chute and on the finish line to determine the proper order in which competitors enter the chute. Their decision is final and without appeal except for possible action taken by the referee or the jury of appeals. (As noted earlier, the jury of appeals is often comprised of a head coach from each team, the meet director and sometimes a student-athlete. The jury doesn't convene unless an appeal is made.)

Chute Director

The chute director supervises the finish chute. This includes directing gate controllers when more than one chute is used, directing marshals to keep the chute area free of unauthorized individuals and assigning positions for chute umpires and any other personnel. It might be necessary to assign stand-ins to take the place of any runner unable to pass through the chute.

Chute Umpires and Callers

The chute umpires supervise the runners after they enter the chute and ensure they are properly checked to prevent an irregularity in the order of finish. The chute umpires see that all runners who cross the finish line are given their proper order as they proceed through the chute.

The caller calls the number of each runner in the order of his or her proper place in the chute. The caller provides this information to finish-line checkers, which helps ensure that the finish order doesn't get mixed up.

Checkers

Checkers keep a record of the runners and their order of the finish as announced by the caller. In a case of a conflict, if two checkers are in agreement, their records are accepted. If an agreement can't be reached by at least two checkers, the referee makes the final decision.

An additional checker might record the order of finish using a tape recorder, a procedure that serves as a back-up in case a problem occurs. Checkers also sometimes use numbered cards. A card—or finish ticket—with a number indicating the order of finish is handed to each competitor on leaving the chute. (Note that finish-line tickets are fast becoming obsolete because meet directors are going to bar codes or computer chips to record finish places.)

Numbers Manager

A competitor must wear the assigned, unaltered number when numbers are used. The numbers manager ensures the competitors' numbers are placed in the proper team packet and reports any missing number or irregularity to the table at which entries are confirmed.

As you can see, a tremendous amount of work goes into the administration of track and field and cross country meets. In this chapter you've learned the essential responsibilities and procedures of administering meets in both sports; in the next chapter we'll cover the duties and mechanics of officials conducting the running events for a track and field meet.

PART II

OFFICIATING MECHANICS

CHAPTER 3

TRACK & FIELD: RUNNING EVENTS

The running events, hurdles and relays involve many athletes—and officials. In this chapter we'll examine the duties and mechanics of officials specific to running events.

Running Event Procedures and Responsibilities

As noted in chapter 2, a referee, a jury of appeals and an inspector of implements head the overall administration of a track and field meet. The officials involved in the running events are

- a running referee;
- a clerk of the course and assistant clerks;
- a starter, assistant starters and lap counters;
- a head finish judge, finish judges and finish-line recorders;
- a head timer and timers;
- a chief finish evaluator, timing operator, wind gauge operator; and
- a head umpire and umpires.

Running Referee

Except for the meet referee, the running referee has more jurisdiction over the running events than any other official. The duties of the running referee are determined by the meet referee, the meet director or the games committee. The running referee is also responsible for inspecting starting blocks unless an inspector of implements has been assigned.

Clerk of the Course

The clerk of the course records the name and number of each competitor and assigns each competitor to the proper heat and starting position, as approved by the games committee or meet director. Either the clerk or the assistant starter should be at the starting area before each race to announce lane assignments and to hold each competitor responsible for reporting promptly to the starting line when the race is announced. The clerk makes adjustments in heat or lane assignments, or in the number of heat qualifiers, with the approval of the referee. In a race run in lanes, each athlete must run in the lane drawn unless the clerk moves the athlete to avoid using a lane that, because of unusual conditions, would unfairly handicap the athlete.

The clerk provides the head finish judge with a written list of all of the starting competitors, their numbers and lane assignments, the number to qualify from the preliminaries and the record for the event. If the referee has approved any changes, the clerk provides them in writing to the head finish judge. The clerk also checks and enforces uniform, visible apparel, jewelry, contestant number and shoe regulations and instructs athletes just prior to the race. Among these instructions are

- the method of qualifying in preliminary and semifinal heats;
- places to be scored;
- the type of stagger to be used in the race (e.g., waterfall, one-turn, two-turn, etc.);
- exchange zone markings, location and color;
- remaining in assigned lanes at the end of the race to aid finish-line personnel in the timing and placing process (with contestant number in full view); and
- not to wear prohibited items such as jewelry, hats, baseball caps, bandannas, unapproved sunglasses, kerchiefs, costumes or other special adornments as designated by the games committee.

The clerk needs to inspect or distribute batons for relay races and, following the race, collect (or oversee the collection of) batons from the anchor runners. The clerk must be familiar with all starting and finish lines and exchange zones (see figure 3.1). He or she should coordinate calls with the announcer and assist in keeping the meet on schedule.

To assist in his or her duties, the clerk should be equipped with the following items:

- Time schedule and order of events
- List of entries, heat and lane assignments, event cards

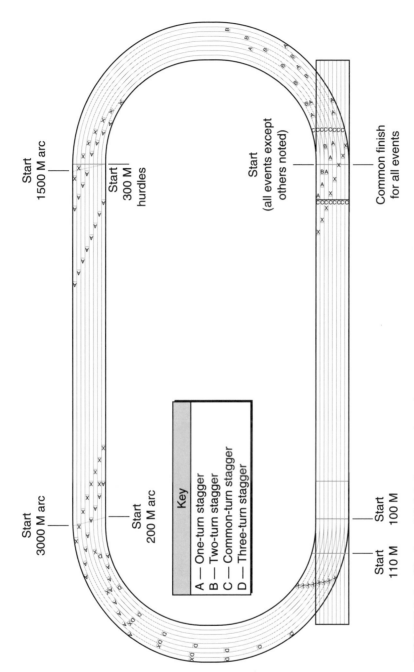

Start
1500 M arc

Start
300 M
hurdles

Start
3000 M arc

Start
200 M arc

Start
(all events except
others noted)

Key

A — One-turn stagger
B — Two-turn stagger
C — Common-turn stagger
D — Three-turn stagger

Start
110 M

Start
100 M

Common finish
for all events

FIGURE 3.1   Start and finish lines and exchange zones.

- Clipboard and pencils
- A watch that has been synchronized with the official meet time
- A speaker system to call missing athletes or teams
- Numbered tongue depressors, balls or discs for drawing for lanes (for small meets)
- A walkie-talkie or radio for communicating with the announcer and finish-line personnel
- Hip numbers (if used)

Sample Event Card

A clerk's best friend can be an event card. Such a card helps the clerk deliver the appropriate instructions for the event and refreshes his or her memory about the particulars of the event's rules. Here is a sample event card for the 400-meter run:

400-meter run

- Two-turn stagger start
- Runners run in assigned lanes all the way
- On a curve, three consecutive steps on or over the line to their left equals disqualification
- Running against time—the six fastest times place and score
- Runners come back to the finish line in their respective lanes to help the judges in their decisions

Starter

The starter has jurisdiction over the competitors at the starting line, once they have been turned over by the clerk. The starter uses the starting device—either a voice amplification device, an electronic sound system or a blank pistol (or a sound equivalent to a .32-caliber pistol outside or a .22-caliber pistol inside). The starter decides, without appeal, whether a start is fair and legal. If a false start occurs, the starter determines which runner (or runners) is to be charged with the false start.

Starters are equipped with a starting device, black powder or pyro shells (if needed), a brightly colored sleeve worn on the arm holding the starting device (to ensure the finish-line official can see the arm), a whistle or a voice amplification device (optional), a starter's platform or ladder (optional) and an extra starting device in case of a malfunction.

The general responsibilities of the starter can be divided into four categories: premeet, positioning, prerace and race start.

Premeet Responsibilities

Before a meet, the starter inspects and tests the starting and timing devices to be used and becomes familiar with the start and finish lines, relay staggers, exchange zones and break-line flags or cones to ensure everything is in place and appropriate (see figure 3.2).

The starter should meet with several individuals before the meet begins:

- The announcer, to confirm the meet time and the schedule for preliminary calls
- The head finish judge, to confirm starting and finishing procedures

FIGURE 3.2   The starter should discuss lane assignments and recall procedures with assistant starters before the meet begins.

- The clerk of the course, to clarify the prerace instructions to be provided to the athletes (so that information doesn't overlap)
- The assistant starter, to discuss recall procedures

Positioning

The positioning of the starters depends on the size of meet, depth of stagger, radius of track and number of officials. As a guiding principle, recall starters should take positions in or near the starter's field of vision, while ensuring they have a clear view of the lanes they are to observe. While the positions and lane responsibilities that follow are generally the best way to guarantee fair starts, a good starting team should always communicate and be ready to make changes under different circumstances. For example, when three starters are covering a heat with only five competitors, they should be able to quickly adapt their positions and lane responsibilities.

Two Starters

If there are two starters—the starter and one recall starter—they should position as shown in figure 3.3. The recall starter has the same responsibility as the starter in ensuring a fair start; he or she can stop a race and recall the competitors if the start is unfair. Here are the positions and mechanics for the starter and recall starter when two starters are used for a race:

- *Starter.* Stands on the inside of the track midway between the inside and outside runner and provides the start commands to the runners after hand signals are provided from the recall starter. The starter is primarily responsible for lanes 5 through 8 for false starts and any block slippage.

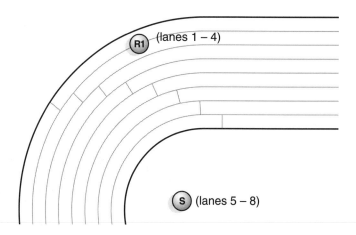

FIGURE 3.3   Positioning for two starters.

- *Recall starter.* Stands in or near lane 8, directly across from the starter approximately even with the lane 4 start line and provides hand signals to the starter when runners are ready for the "Set!" command (see figure 3.7 on page 50). The recall starter is primarily responsible for observing lanes 1 through 4 for false starts and block slippage.

Three Starters

In bigger competitions, three starters are often used to ensure a fair start by all competitors. In such a case, there are a starter and two recall starters. For starter positioning, see figure 3.4. Here's a description of the positioning and mechanics for each starter:

- *Starter.* Stands on the inside of the track an equal distance from the inside and outside runner and provides the start commands to the runners after hand signals are provided from both recall starters. The starter should watch for false starts and block slippages in lanes 4 and 5.

- *Recall starter 1.* Stands in or near lane 8, directly across from the starter approximately even with the lane 4 start line and provides hand signals when runners are ready for the "Set!" command (see figure 3.7 on page 50). Recall starter 1 is responsible for lanes 1 through 3 for false starts and block slippage. He or she should also protect the welfare of the athletes by calling "Up!" if a delay keeps them in the blocks too long.

- *Recall starter 2.* Stands in or near the outside lanes, observing lanes 6 through 8 for false starts and block slippage. Recall starter 2 provides hand signals when runners are ready for the "Set!" command.

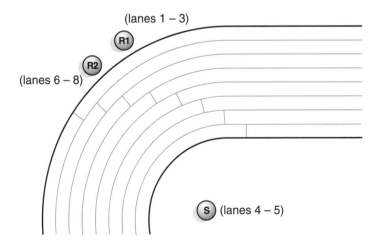

FIGURE 3.4 Positioning for three starters on a three- or four-turn stagger.

For races with one- or two-turn staggers, where the runners are closer together, recall starter 2 may have a poor view of block slippage and false starts in the outside lanes. If so, the starter and recall starter 2 should swap lane assignments while staying in or near the regular three-starter positions. Recall starter 2 observes the middle lanes, while the starter observes the outside lanes and both recall starters.

Four Starters

Some large competitions use four starters. The advantage here is that each starter can focus on fewer lanes, making it easier to detect a false start. When there are four starters, including three recall starters, they should position as shown in figure 3.5. Here's a description of the positioning and mechanics for each starter:

- *Starter.* Stands 15 to 30 feet on the inside of the track at an equal distance from all runners and provides the start commands to the runners after hand signals are provided from recall starter 3. The starter should watch for false starts and block slippages in all lanes, although this duty is primarily covered by the recall starters.

- *Recall starter 1.* Stands in lane 5 or 6 approximately even with the lane 3 start line and provides hand signals to recall starter 2 when runners are ready for the "Set!" command (see figure 3.7 on page 50). Recall starter 1 is responsible for observing lanes 1 through 3 for false starts and block slippage.

- *Recall starter 2.* Stands in lane 6 or 7 approximately even with the lane 6 start line and provides a hand signal to recall starter 3. Recall starter 2 is responsible for observing lanes 3 through 5 for false starts and block slippage.

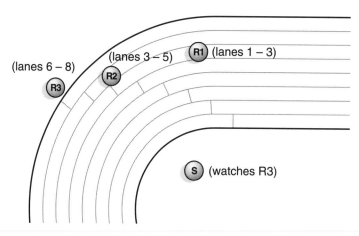

FIGURE 3.5   Positioning for four starters.

- *Recall starter 3.* Stands outside of lane 8 approximately even with the lane 8 start line and provides a hand signal to the starter after receiving a signal from recall starter 2. Recall starter 3 is responsible for observing lanes 6 through 8 for false starts and block slippage.

Straight Lanes

For races run in straight lanes, the starter and three recall officials should position as shown in figure 3.6. Here are position and mechanics descriptions for straightaway positions:

- *Starter.* Stands 8 to 20 feet in front of the start line extension. The starter is responsible for false starts only when they aren't called by the recall starters. If only two starters (i.e., starter and recall starter) are working an event, the starter is responsible for observing false starts and block slippage in lanes 1 through 4. If three or four starters are working an event, the starter keeps an overview of all lanes and watches for recall starter 1's signal.
- *Recall starter 1.* Provides inconspicuous hand signals to the starter when the runners are ready for the "Set!" command (see figure 3.7). Recall starter 1 is responsible for lanes 5 through 8 for false starts.
- *Recall starter 2 (if applicable).* Provides hand signals to recall starter 1 and is responsible for watching for false starts and block slippage in lanes 1 through 4.
- *Recall starter 3 (if applicable).* Stands opposite the starter and is responsible for watching for false starts and block slippage in all lanes. Recall starter 3 does not provide hand signals.

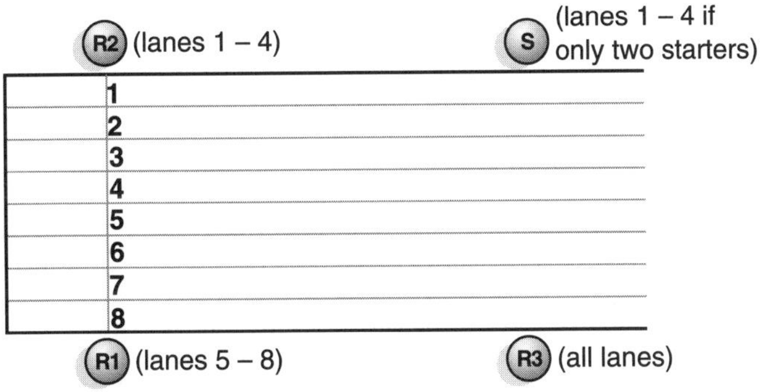

FIGURE 3.6   Straight lanes positioning.

Alley or Distance Lane Starts

For alley or distance lane starts, the starter and recall starters position as shown in figure 3.8. Here are position and mechanics descriptions for alley or distance lane starts:

a   b

FIGURE 3.7 *(a-b)* When runners are in position and ready for the "Set!" command the recall starter should signal with slow, subtle movement so as not to distract them.

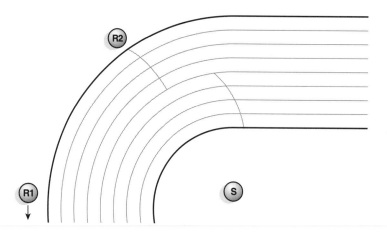

FIGURE 3.8 Alley or distance lane start positioning.

- *Starter.* Stands 5 to 15 feet on the inside of the track at as close to an equal distance from all runners as possible. No hand signals are given by the recall starters.
- *Recall starter 1.* Stands 60 to 80 meters from the start; recalls the race if a runner falls because of contact with another runner.
- *Recall starter 2 (if applicable).* Stands 5 to 10 feet outside of the last runner on the opposite side from the starter; recalls the race if runners are not behind the starting line, motionless, or if a distraction has caused an unfair start when the starting device is fired.

Prerace Duties

Just prior to the race and before giving remaining instructions, the starter should again inspect the starting device to make sure it's ready. Anyone other than the athletes entered in the race are directed by the starter to move away from the starting line. Part of the starter's job is to control the environment around the starting area so athletes can focus on the start of the race. As athletes are preparing for the start, the starter checks the athletes to ensure they're not breaking any uniform or jewelry rules (in most cases, if an athlete is breaking a rule, the starter should give him or her a chance to remedy the situation before the race begins).

One of the starter's main duties before a race is to give final instructions to the athletes. Appropriate instructions might go something like this:

> Runners, do not delay in responding to my commands. At the command, "On your marks," I will give you reasonable time to assume a comfortable position. When the command, "Set!" is given, I'll expect you to promptly come to your final position, not touching the start line and remaining motionless until the starting device is fired. If you hear a series of short whistles or a second shot after the start, halt and return to the starting line.

After giving the instructions, the starter asks the runners if they have any questions. If there are questions, they should be answered as briefly as possible.

When the head finish judge signals with either a whistle or white flag, the starter instructs the competitors to remove their warm-up clothes. The starter then takes a position appropriate for the type of race being run. If not started with a one-turn stagger, races longer than 400 meters can be recalled any time during the first 100 meters.

Starting the Race

To start races or opening relay legs of less than 800 meters, the starter commands, "On your marks!" in a strong voice all runners can easily hear. At command, the athletes immediately take their proper positions behind their starting lines. Once runners are in position and steady on their marks, the next command from the starter is "Set!" At this point, without delay, all athletes assume their full and final set position so that no part of their bodies touches on or over the starting line (see figure 3.9). The interval between the set command and the firing of the starting device is usually one to two seconds. To alert the timers the race is about to begin, the starter raises his or her free hand while giving the set command. (Of course, if a microphone is used, the starter won't have a free hand.)

After the set command, the starter waits until runners are set and motionless, and then fires the device. (Note that assistant starters should keep their finger off the recall device activator during the starter's preliminaries or else it might accidentally be set off.)

For any reason, either before or after the set command, the starter may delay a start by directing all athletes to stand. After appropriate adjustments are made, the starter then goes through the same commands to make a new start.

If a runner fails to comply with the commands of the starter or repeatedly delays in assuming the final position, it is a false start. False starts also occur when a runner touches the ground in front of the starting line with any part of his or her body, or when he or she is in motion prior to firing the starting device. Any runner making a false start is disqualified.

In the following sections are suggestions for starting races in different situations, including when using a public address system, when starting from a crouch, when using stagger or nonstagger starts and when running races of 800 meters or longer.

FIGURE 3.9   A sprinter just after the "Set!" command.

Starting With a Public Address System

When a starter is using a voice amplification system and is holding the microphone in one hand, during the command, "On your marks!" he or she raises the starting device to an overhead position (see figure 3.10) and then lowers it to a horizontal, shoulder-level position. When all runners are comfortable and motionless, the starter raises the device to the fully extended position and immediately gives the "Set!" command. When the runners are set, the starter then fires the device.

Starting From a Crouched Position

In almost all cases, runners begin a sprint or hurdles race from a crouched position (see figure 3.11). In these races, after signaling the head finish judge and the head timer that the race is about to begin and after receiving the

FIGURE 3.10 A starter calling runners to their marks using a public address system.

FIGURE 3.11 Runner in a crouched position at the start.

"ready" signal, the starter raises the starting device to a position overhead and gives the command, "On your marks!"

As the starter gives the "On your marks!" command, he or she swings the other arm, starting with the elbow straight and hand at the side, backward and upward over the head and then down in front, ending with the hand pointing to the ground in front. After the athletes are comfortable and motionless, the command, "Set!" is given as the starter quickly raises his or her free hand overhead (figure 3.12). The starter fires the starting device after observing that all competitors are set and motionless. If this takes too long, the starter calls the athletes up and starts over from the beginning.

Stagger Starts

When the starting marks are staggered for more than one turn, such as for the 400-meter dash (two turns), 400-meter relay (two turns) or the 1,600-meter relay (three turns), the starter should tell the runners whether vocal commands or whistle commands will be used.

If whistle commands are used, the starter positions in front of the runners and outside the race course and gives five or six short blasts on the whistle. This signals athletes to stand at their marks and alerts the timers and judges to be ready. When the head finish judge has signaled "ready" (by waving a white flag or blowing a whistle), the starter raises the starting device overhead (see figure 3.13a on page 56) and gives one long blast on the whistle while swinging his or her free arm, starting with the elbow straight and hand at the side, backward and upward overhead (see figure 3.13b on page 56). The arm is then brought down in front, ending with the hand pointed to the ground. This is the signal for all competitors to get on their marks.

After a reasonable delay, the starter sounds another long blast on the whistle while raising his or her free arm overhead. This signals runners to assume their set position. When all runners are set and motionless, the starter fires the starting device. If the starter needs to call runners off their mark, he or she gives the whistle five or six short blasts and moves an arm in front of the body. (Note that the directions for whistle signals are meant to be used only when a voice amplification system is not available. Whistle starts can be confusing; voice amplification systems are preferred and should be used whenever possible.)

Nonstagger Starts

For nonstagger starts, the starter positions five to eight yards ahead of the starting line inside or outside the track (see starter position in figure 3.6 on page 49). Prior to the set command, the starter observes the entire starting area. After the set command, the starter focuses on the competitors.

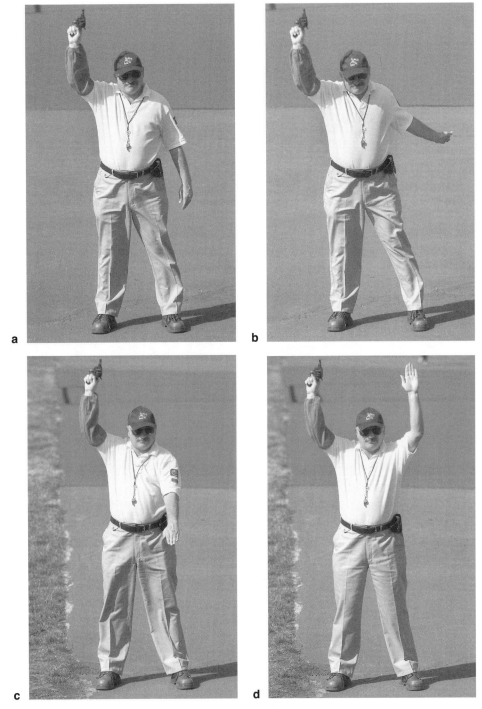

FIGURE 3.12 *(a)* A starter with the device overhead and other arm down at the side, *(b)* other arm going backward and upward overhead, *(c)* in final position with hand pointing to the ground in front, and *(d)* with free hand raised overhead, ready to start the race.

a   b

FIGURE 3.13 *(a)* Starter swinging free arm with elbow straight and hand at side and *(b)* starter with starting device overhead and whistle in mouth.

Races of 800 Meters and Longer

In individual races or relay races of 800 meters or longer, starters use only one vocal command: "On your marks!" After signaling the head finish judge and head timer and receiving the "all ready" signal, but prior to the "On your marks!" command, the starter raises the starting device overhead with one hand and with the other hand points to the ground in front of him or her.

To alleviate the problem of runners leaning or moving at the starting line on the set command, the starter should instruct all competitors to take a position one or more steps behind the starting line—or on the dashed arc behind the line, if there is one. On the command, "On your marks!" runners should immediately step to the starting line as the starter raises his or her arm overhead. When all runners are set and motionless, the starter fires the starting device.

Assistant Starter

The assistant starter helps the starter in his or her duties, including ensuring a fair start. The assistant starter can stop the race and recall the runners if he or she observes an unfair start. Assistant starters are especially recommended for staggered starts, when it's difficult for one starter to observe all competitors. If a runner falls during the first 100 meters as a result of contact with another runner in a race of 400 meters or more, or in the first 100 meters of the first leg of any relay, the recall device should be fired and the race restarted. Most falls are caused by contact, whether the contact is seen or not, and usually disrupts other runners. Within the first 100 meters and when the cause of a fall is unknown, it's usually best to stop and restart the race.

Halting the Starting Process

When a situation that prevents a fair start for all competitors is observed, the assistant starter should halt the starting process by loudly blowing a whistle in a series of short blasts. The clerk of the course should have told the runners that short whistle blasts mean the starting procedure is being aborted and that they can come out of their starting position without penalty.

Sometimes the starter might not be aware of a situation that could prevent a fair start. In such cases, it becomes very important for the assistant starter to take charge. Here's a list of situations in which an assistant starter should halt the starting process:

- When there are distractions in the starting area
- When a clicking camera or another sound might stimulate a start
- When the runners are lining up at an incorrect starting line
- When one or more athletes is experiencing starting block problems
- When people or objects are coming onto the track
- When the starter is moving ahead in the starting sequence before all competitors are ready
- When one or more runners are having trouble holding the set position because of a lack of balance or strength (not because of rolling through the set position)
- When technical problems occur (e.g., incorrect lane position, timing or meet official difficulties, announcer interference)
- When a red flag is waved by a finish judge or by the FAT operator

- When one or more competitors false start before the starter fires the starting device (When this occurs, call the athletes up in a relaxed manner rather than firing the starting device and then firing it again to indicate a false start. Don't, however, call the athletes up to "save" a competitor who is using a rolling technique from committing a false start. Only call them up after a false start has been committed.)

Umpires

The head umpire supervises the assistant umpires and positions them in the best place for them to carry out their responsibilities. Umpires report race irregularities to the head umpire, and the head umpire reports directly to the referee, who makes final decisions. The head umpire also provides marking material to relay exchange-zone umpires. Before any hurdle race, the head umpire indicates to the finish-line recorder (by holding up a white flag) that the hurdles are properly set. The finish-line coordinator (head finish judge) then signals to the starter that the race can begin.

During a race, umpires should remain at their stations until the race is completed. Each umpire has a white flag, a yellow flag, violation reports and a pen or pencil. At the end of the race, assistant umpires should remove tape or markings from the track and check in with the head umpire at a designated place before the next race starts.

As runners pass umpires at their stations, umpires wave a white flag if they observe no infraction. If they do observe an infraction, they should do the following:

- Wave a yellow flag to indicate a possible violation.
- Record the number of the competitor who committed the foul, their assigned lane, the uniform color and, if possible, the school of the competitor who was fouled. They then complete and sign a violation report (see "Violation Report" and "Summary of Running Rules Infractions Reporting Form" in appendix A on pages 135 and 136) to give to the head umpire.
- Remain at their position until the race is over and then report to the head umpire.
- Refrain from discussing the possible infraction with coaches, athletes or spectators until the referee has made a decision on the matter. (In fact, it's best to not discuss infractions with these groups at all.)

After a race in which a violation has occurred, either the head umpire or the referee should tell the head finish judge and announcer not to announce results until the referee has made a final decision. In meets in which a jury of appeals renders the final decision, the announcement may be delayed until the jury reaches a judgment.

Positioning

Umpires position according to their assignments and the particular race being run. Figure 3.14 shows proper umpire positioning for a 400-meter run. The head umpire should provide a copy of the appropriate form to each assistant umpire for each event.

When lanes extend around a turn, umpires position so they can collectively observe the entire turn. Each umpire on a turn near the finish line should move toward the finish line as the race is ending and watch for possible infractions.

Positioning specifications for umpires for various races are described in the sections that follow. All umpires should be available for all races.

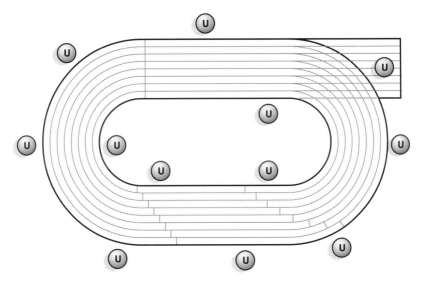

FIGURE 3.14   Umpire positioning for a 400-meter race.

100-Meter Dash and 100- and 110-Meter Hurdles

Umpires in two teams station between the start and finish lines, with one team on each side of the track. Each team is responsible for half of the track; for instance, on an eight-lane track, one team is responsible for lanes 1, 2, 3 and 4, and the second team is responsible for lanes 5, 6, 7 and 8 (see figure 3.15).

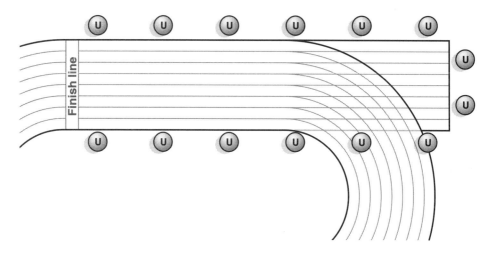

FIGURE 3.15   Umpire positioning for a 100-meter dash.

300-Meter Hurdles

The umpires have the additional responsibility of judging whether competitors are clearing hurdles legally. Since the hurdles are staggered and placed around a turn, there is a high potential for competitors to go partially around a hurdle, or to cause a lane infraction after they clear a hurdle. Umpires in this event are separated into an infield team and an outfield team, and positioned so they can collectively observe the entire turn while paying close attention to all hurdle attempts. After the runners have cleared the last turn, umpires near this turn should move toward the finish and continue to watch for possible infractions (see figure 3.16).

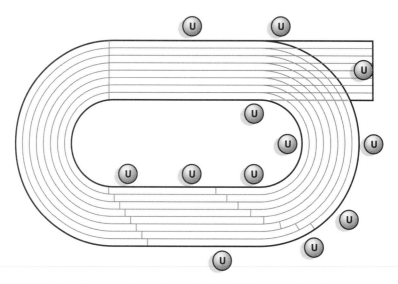

FIGURE 3.16   Positioning of umpires for the 300-meter hurdles.

Staggered Races

For races that are staggered for the first turn only, the head umpire should be near the referee and in position to observe the entire race:

One-stagger races are generally 800 meters or longer, in which the runners "cut to the pole" at a designated location. On a 400-meter track, a one-turn stagger is also used for the 200-meter dash (see figure 3.17a) and 300-meter hurdles (both races are run in lanes all the way). A two-turn stagger is used for the 400-meter dash and 400-meter relay (again, both races are run in lanes all the way), as shown in figure 3.17b.

A three-turn stagger is recommended for the 1,600-meter (4 × 400) relay, with the first runners running in lanes all the way and the second

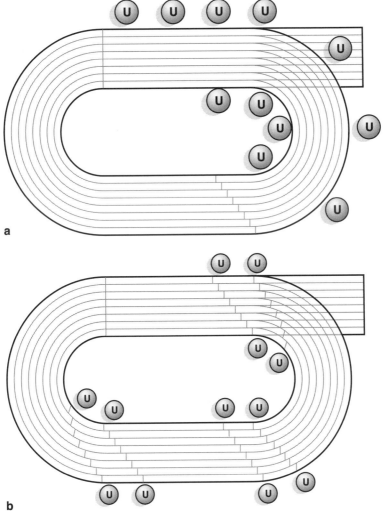

a

b

FIGURE 3.17   Positioning of umpires for a *(a)* 200-meter dash and *(b)* 400-meter relay.

runners cutting to the pole after one turn. The three-turn stagger is also recommended for the sprint medley (400-200-200-800).

A four-turn stagger is used for the 800-meter relay, run in lanes all the way. A box-alley, one-turn stagger has become popular for races beyond 800 meters. This helps to avoid crowding and the potential disqualifications for interference that can more easily occur when a waterfall start (all runners bunched together) is used.

Lap Counters

The lap counter is either the referee or someone else appointed to count laps. In races or relay legs of more than three laps, it's the responsibility of lap counters to inform the runners (either by calling out or using a signal) the number of laps they have left before the finish. Keeping track of laps can get quite confusing in longer races, when slower runners are lapped, sometimes more than once. The lap counter must concentrate on the race and not be distracted. In long races with many competitors, it's a good idea to appoint several lap counters to assist in keeping track of the athletes.

Timers

The head timer is in charge of the assistant timers. The head timer is responsible for determining the winning time for each running event and records times for all place-winners as established by the games committee. The head timer or a designated assistant timer calls out lap times in distance races.

Assistant timers support the head timer. In addition to the head timer, two assistant timers and one backup timer also time first place. The time recorded by the backup timer is used only when one of the three regular timers fails to record a time for an event. Assistant timers can time other places as well. The ideal is to have three timers for each place, but it's generally difficult to find enough timers for most high school meets, especially for dual meets or triangulars. In such cases, finish-line judges do double duty as timers. When finish-line judges time races, their priority is order of finish first and timing second.

Timers position inside or outside the track at the finish line, preferably on an elevated platform that allows timers standing behind them to see the finish clearly. If fully automatic timing (FAT) is used, the head timer and assistants serve as backup timers in case the system malfunctions. The head timer consults with the FAT operator and confirms the official winning times for all place-winners or all competitors following each race. When FAT is used, the games committee might reduce or even eliminate the use of timers at the finish line.

Before a meet in which a FAT system won't be used, the timer should come to the meet having thoroughly reviewed the rules concerning timing. The timer's watch should be secured, with the lanyard around his or her neck. The timer should test start and stop the watch to ensure familiarity with the watch before race time. Typically, the timer cradles the watch in his or her palm and uses the same hand's index finger to start and stop it.

When preparing to time a race, the timer ensures the watch has been reset. When the starter signals that the race is about to start, the head timer directs the assistants to check their watches. When the athletes go to their marks, the head timer says, "Device up," and all talking at the finish line ceases.

At this point, the timer focuses undivided attention on the starter's starting device. The watch should start at once with the flash or smoke of the starting device. If for some reason a timer isn't able to start his or her watch with the flash, he or she should immediately notify the head timer and the substitute timer so that the substitute's watch becomes the official clock. When a false start occurs, the head timer instructs all assistant timers to reset their watches.

As the athletes approach the finish line, the timer focuses on the line, stopping the watch when any part of the runner's torso (not the head, arms, legs, feet or hands) reaches the edge of the finish line (see figure 3.18).

FIGURE 3.18 Runner in full stride whose hand or arm is across the finish line but whose torso has not yet crossed. This runner has not yet officially reached the finish line.

The timer retains attention on the finish line, even if a runner falls down. A runner who falls and crawls or rolls across the finish line finishes when any part of the torso has crossed the finish line. The entire body need not cross the line.

After a race, timers don't reset their watches until they're sure the head timer and referee have confirmed the official time and recorded it. At the conclusion of the meet, all watches are returned to the head timer.

Chief Finish Evaluator

The chief finish evaluator is in charge of the FAT device. As mentioned, when FAT is used, the games committee might reduce or eliminate the use of timers at the finish line. When a FAT system and timers are both used, the FAT system takes precedence over handheld times.

The chief finish evaluator records the finish time automatically when any part of the runner's torso reaches the perpendicular plane of the nearer edge of the finish line. Time shall be recorded in one 100th of a second. When determining a subsequent round, timing to one 1,000th of a second might be used.

Finish Judges

At least two assistant finish judges should be assigned for each place to be scored. The head finish judge views the finish of the race as a whole and designates at which place each assistant finish judge will focus. Should a place-winner be overlooked, the head finish judge, based on his or her observation, may correctly place the athlete. This happens only if the other judges can't resolve the matter.

Assistant judges should position on opposite sides of the track, if possible. They should stand about 20 feet back from, and in direct line with, the finish line (see figure 3.19). Their decisions are final and without appeal except for possible action taken by the head finish judge, referee or jury of appeals. The games committee can reduce or eliminate the use of finish judges if FAT is used.

In their championship meets, most state associations use a FAT device that provides a photo or video of the finish of each race. (FAT is also used in many invitational meets.) In meets where FAT is used, the picture becomes the official record of the race, and the finish judges' decisions are used only in case of malfunction of the electronic device. The games committee or meet director designates a procedure to follow when the FAT system malfunctions. When this device is used, the head finish judge should consult with the chief finish evaluator following each race to confirm the official order of finish, unless the evaluator is in a booth far from the finish line.

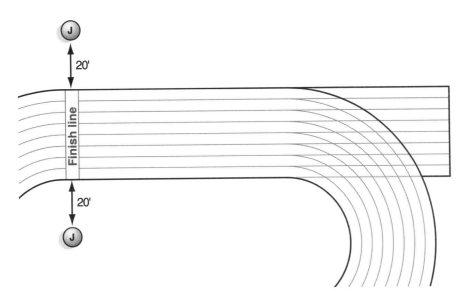

FIGURE 3.19 Proper positioning of assistant finish judges.

Premeet Responsibilities

Before the meet, the head finish judge ensures he or she is thoroughly familiar with the rules concerning all aspects of each running event. The head finish judge reports to the meet director at least 45 minutes before the first running event and picks up a flag and enough finish pads, pencils and whistles for all the judges.

The head finish judge meets with assistant judges 30 minutes before the event and assigns two judges for each place and for the first nonplacing position. The head finish judge passes out the finish slips and pencils to the assistants and assigns them their positions, placing them on either side of the track and, if possible, in a direct line with the finish line.

In addition to this meeting, the head finish judge and the other judges—as well as other finish-line personnel—confer with the meet referee before the start of the meet for the "finish-line briefing."

The head finish judge should always know where the referee is in case there's a need to confer with him or her after a race. Following the race, the head finish judge collects the finish slips and the wind gauge reading, and, after checking them, gives them to the finish-line recorder, verifying with the recorder that there are no disqualifications.

Meet Responsibilities

The head finish judge ensures all assistant judges, times and pickers are ready before each race. If FAT is being used, the head finish judge watches for the FAT operator's flag signals (a white flag means the timer is ready; a red flag means the timer is not ready). The head finish judge

---

Finish-Line Briefing

The meet referee should cover the following items in a premeet conference with all finish-line personnel:

- Rules governing the finish
- Reporting and recording procedures
- Handling discrepancies in timing or order of finish
- Prerace instructions given by the clerk of the course to athletes about
  postrace finish-line procedures
- Handling disqualifications as they affect the final order of finish
- The role and authority of each type of official
- Individual assignments, officials' positions, equipment distribution
  and return
- The use of judges and timers at the finish line if a FAT system is
  used

---

signals the starter by holding a white flag up or blowing a whistle when
finish-line officials are ready. In many cases, the head finish judge has
access to walkie-talkies, which makes communication easier.

All assistant finish judges should have their place slips with event
numbers before the start of the race. Assistant finish judges give their
full attention to the race as the head judge signals the starter. During
the race, the assistant finish judge focuses on all runners until they're
within 10 meters of the finish line, at which point the focus shifts to the
finish line. The assistant finish judge selects the place he or she has been
assigned as the athletes cross the finish line.

As is the case for the timers, assistant finish judges must remember
that if a runner falls before reaching the finish, their focus must remain
on the finish line as they ensure the runner's torso reaches the edge of the
line before a finish is recorded. At the conclusion of the race, the assistant
finish judge writes his or her decision on the place slip and, without
consulting anyone, hands the slip to the head finish judge.

Finish-Line Recorder

The finish-line recorder's duties involve recording times and places. Many
times this function is performed by the head finish judge or another judge
appointed by the head finish judge. The finish-line recorder positions near
the finish line, in clear view of the line and the competitors. He or she

is responsible for recording the official order of finish of all qualifiers or place-winners from results submitted by the head finish judge, recording times as submitted by the head timer, recording anemometer readings when applicable and delivering race results to the official scorer.

Wind Gauge Operator

Anemometer readings to measure wind velocity are used to validate record performance in events up to and including 200 meters plus the long and triple jumps. Here we'll discuss the running events only; in the next chapter we'll cover the wind gauge operator's procedures during the long and triple jumps.

The wind gauge operator should have a schedule of events so he or she knows the timing of the events in which readings are required. For the 100-meter dash and for the 100- and 110-meter hurdles, the wind gauge operator positions midway between the start and finish lines and measures the wind velocity from start to finish. For 200-meter races, the best position is midway between the beginning of the straightaway and the finish line, from which point wind velocity is measured for 10 seconds, beginning as the runners enter the straightaway.

Regardless of the event, the wind gauge operator should position the wind gauge within two meters of the track and 1.22 meters (4 feet) high. The anemometer should face the starting line in order to measure any favoring wind. Readings should be recorded after each race.

Wind recordings are necessary only to measure the speed of wind blowing in the direction of the runners—that is, a wind that aids performance. The maximum allowable average wind velocity is 4.473 miles per hour (or two meters per second).

It takes many officials, and a lot of expertise, to conduct the variety of running events in a track and field meet. Even if you usually operate within a particular area of officiating, you should be familiar with the procedures and mechanics for all officials, including how they interact with each other. So, study this chapter well and use it as a reference as you prepare to officiate running events. In the next chapter we'll cover similar territory for the field events of a track and field meet.

CHAPTER 4

TRACK & FIELD: FIELD EVENTS

As is the case with the running events, field events require a number of officials accepting several responsibilities to conduct the field portion of a track and field meet smoothly. In this chapter we'll look at the duties and mechanics of field officials, examine how to break ties in field events and take an event-by-event look at how to conduct the field events.

Field Events Procedures and Responsibilities

The officials that administer the field events are listed here:

- Head field referee or head field judge
- Inspector of implements and assistants
- Field judges (head judges and assistants) for the discus, shot put and javelin; the high jump; and the long jump and triple jump
- Wind gauge operator

Head Field Referee

Field referees are responsible for the conduct and supervision of the field events. The responsibilities of the head field referee include the following:

- Reviewing procedures for using equipment and implements
- Inspecting apparatuses, such as crossbars, jumping standards, pits and so on, to ensure they are legal, in place and ready for the event to begin (see "Field Event Checklist" in appendix A on page 138)
- Conducting a premeet meeting of all individual event judges
- Ensuring field events begin on time and continue without unnecessary delay

- Ensuring each competitor has a fair and equal opportunity to perform
- Verifying performances that might qualify for records
- Reviewing and certifying scorecards for each completed field event
- Instructing event judges to secure facilities and return equipment after completing competition
- Communicating with the meet referee, as necessary

Field Judge Meeting

The field referee should cover each of the following items in a premeet conference with all field judges:

- The role and authority of field judges
- Rules governing the events, including legal attempts, fouls and measurements
- Pre-event instructions given by the field judges to the competitors
- Breaking ties
- Reporting and recording procedures
- Individual assignments, judges' positions during the events, equipment distribution and return
- Procedure for excusing a competitor to check into a running event

Inspector of Implements

The implement inspector is under the supervision of the meet referee and the field referee. The implement inspector weighs, measures and certifies all implements to be used in competition (e.g., shot puts, javelins, discs, vaulting poles, starting blocks). The implements that have passed inspection are marked so that everyone knows they're legal and have been checked. Any illegal implements discovered are impounded and released to the team's coach after the event has ended.

For the pole vault, the inspector should be sure to check the manufacturer's pole rating and make sure the weight of the vaulter is within the recommended limits. For running events, starting blocks must be inspected to ensure they are within specifications.

Field Judges

The individual event field judges report to the field referee. Field judges should report to the event site at least 45 minutes before the event is scheduled to begin. All field judges attend the premeet field judge meeting to review their assignments and those of others working in the same event.

Field judges must check their competition area to ensure it's officially ready and open for warm-ups. All hard and unyielding surfaces around the high-jump and pole-vault landing pads must be properly padded; no metal crossbars are allowed and vaulting standards must be securely fastened.

Competitors should be checked in by the field judge early enough to have time to complete warm-ups before their event starts; as they are checked in, the field judge enforces uniform, jewelry, visible apparel and shoe regulations.

Competitors should be kept out of the event area during warm-ups and competition; use traffic control ropes, flags or fences around the competition area to help keep the competition area clear of all nonparticipating individuals.

The field judge conducts the trials according to the procedure established by the games committee, including when and how athletes are excused to compete in another event. During the competition, the field judge calls the contestants "up," "on deck" and "on hold" (e.g., "Jenkins up, Terrell on deck, Schmidt on hold"). An assistant should carry implements out of the landing sector to the athlete in the waiting area. The implements should never be thrown back from the field to the waiting or throwing area.

If an athlete's trial hasn't been initiated within the defined time period after the athlete has been called, the athlete should be charged with an unsuccessful trial. The field judge uses a white flag to indicate a fair trial and a red flag to indicate a foul trial.

Following a trial, a competitor should be under control before leaving the circle or javelin runway. This means he or she has regained and can maintain balance. The field judge should ensure the competitor doesn't leave the circle or javelin runway before the implement has landed (if the event is a throw) and the "mark" has been called. After a distance is measured, the field judge announces the distance in a loud, clear voice so athletes and coaches in the vicinity can hear it. A speaker system or amplifier is recommended.

After the event is over, the field judge signs the event card, indicating the place-winners. No athletes should be permitted to linger or practice in an event area; all implements should be removed from the area and a traffic cone (or similar object) placed in position to indicate the area is closed.

Discus Judges

The discus judge is concerned with ensuring the discus throw area and cage are appropriate for competition; checking if the athletes are following the rules regarding uniforms, jewelry, belts and any tape worn; judging whether throws are legal or not; and measuring legal throws. If a performance board is used to display athletes' scores, the discus judge also needs to ensure that information is accurately recorded on the board. Three discus judges and three assistants should be present at the competition, positioned as shown in figure 4.1. Divide the responsibilities this way:

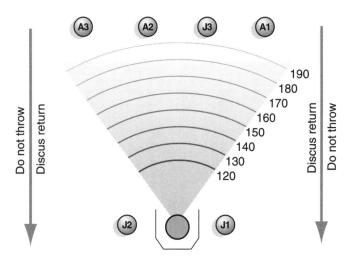

FIGURE 4.1   Position of discus judges and assistants.

- *Judge 1*. Rules on all trials, records each measurement, calls throwing order, judges ring fouls.
- *Judge 2*. Responds to the command by judge 1 to "mark" by conducting measurements, enforces time limits and helps judge 1 look for ring fouls.
- *Judge 3*. Determines impact point and conducts measurements with judge 2.
- *Assistants*. Help determine impact points and carry each discus beyond the throwing sector and back to the throwing area. A discus should never be thrown back. If assistants are not helping mark the impact, they should be outside the sector lines until the implement lands.

Discus Throw Area and Cage Specifications

Whether portable or permanent, the discus cage should be made of heavy nylon netting or another material that absorbs the energy of the discus, preventing any bounce-back. The cage should have both rear and side netting that extends forward to at least the front of the ring (and preferably several feet beyond the front of the ring). The cage offers limited safety to officials, athletes and spectators in the immediate throwing area, but it doesn't ensure everyone's safety. Judges should take caution while officiating the discus event. Cage specifications are shown in figure 4.2.

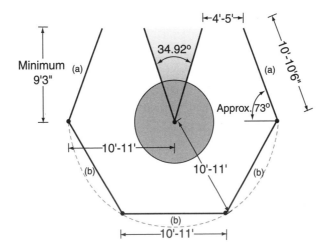

FIGURE 4.2   Discus cage specifications.

When the discus is contested on the track infield, and the cage has a 40-degree sector or 34.92-degree sector (rather than the 60-degree sector shown in figure 4.2), the ends of the cage must be moved to within four to five feet of the sector lines. You can use a moveable front gate to adjust to the degrees of the sector. The specifications for the discus cage are as follows:

- Height: 10 to 12 feet
- Distance from corner post to sector line: 4 to 5 feet
- Distance from center of circle to fencing: 10 to 11 feet
- Fencing: placed 10 feet by 10 feet, 6 inches on the sides and 10 to 11 feet to the rear of the cage

Legal Throw

A thrower may use only a legal discus and can't use reference marks within the circle. A legal throw is made from within the circle and lands within the sector. A thrower may interrupt an attempt and exit and re-enter the circle from either the front or the back half, as long as this occurs within the time limit and the thrower is physically under control. The thrower must exit from the rear half of the circle after the "mark" command has been called by the head judge.

Foul Throw

Fouls can be committed by discus throwers in several ways. If throwers do any of the following, a foul is called:

- After stepping into the circle, they don't pause before starting the throw.
- After stepping into the circle, they touch the circle with any part of their bodies during a throw. (This doesn't include the inner face of the band, if one is used.)
- They throw the discus so that it lands on or outside the sector lines.
- They throw the discus so it hits the cage or hits an object outside the sector and lands within the sector.
- They don't exit through the back half of the circle after the discus has landed and the event judge has called, "Mark!"
- They aren't under control before exiting the circle.
- They don't initiate a trial which is completed within one minute after being called.

If a thrower fouls during a throwing attempt, the discus judge should note the foul by immediately raising a red flag.

Measuring Throws

A legal discus throw is measured from the nearest edge of the first mark made by the discus to the inside edge of the throwing circle nearest the mark (see figure 4.3). The throw should be measured along an extended radius of the circle. The measurement should be recorded to the nearest lesser inch or even-numbered centimeter.

Shot-Put Judges

The shot-put judge assesses athletes to ensure they're not using illegal throwing aids, determines whether puts are legal (see sector specifications shown in figure 4.4) and measures the attempts of each shot putter.

FIGURE 4.3   Measuring a discus throw.

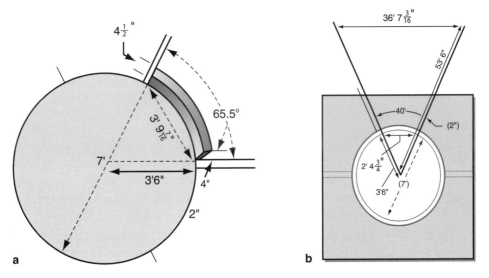

FIGURE 4.4   (*a and b*) Sector specifications for shot put.

Three judges and two assistants should work at the shot-put site and are positioned as shown in figure 4.5. Responsibilities are typically assigned this way:

- *Judge 1.* Rules on all trials, records each measurement, calls the throwing order, judges ring fouls.
- *Judge 2.* Responds to the command by judge 1 to "mark" by conducting measurements, enforces time limits, helps judge ring fouls.

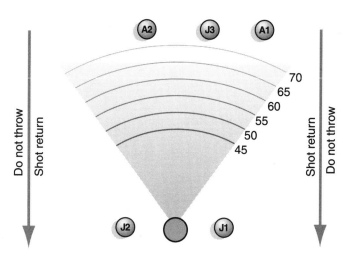

FIGURE 4.5   Officials' positioning for shot put.

- *Judge 3.* Determines impact points and conducts measurements with judge 2.
- *Assistants.* Help determine impact points and carry the shots outside the sector and back to the throwing area. The shots should never be thrown back. If assistants are not helping mark the impact, they should be outside the sector lines until the implement lands.

Legal Put

A legal put is made from within the circle and lands within the sector. An athlete must make a put from the shoulder, with one hand only, so that during the attempt, the shot doesn't drop behind or below the shoulder. Shot putters start from a stationary position inside the circle and cannot attach harnesses or mechanical devices to their hands or arms.

A shot putter can enter the circle from any direction but must exit from the back half. He or she may interrupt an attempt and exit and reenter the circle from the back half, as long as this occurs within the time limit and the athlete is physically under control. A legal shot put must be used, and reference marks are allowed within the circle.

Foul Put

Shot putters can commit fouls in several ways. If putters do any of the following during the shot put, a foul is called:

- After stepping into the circle, they don't pause before starting the throw.

- After stepping into the circle, they touch the circle with any part of their bodies while putting the shot. (This doesn't include the inner face of the stopboard or the band, if one is used.)
- They put the shot so that it lands on or outside the sector lines.
- They put the shot so it hits the cage or hits an object outside the sector and lands within the sector.
- They don't exit through the back half of the circle after the shot has landed and the event judge has called, "Mark!"
- They aren't under control (in balance) before exiting the circle.
- They don't initiate a trial that's completed within one minute after being called.

Measuring Puts

Legal puts are measured from the nearest edge of the first mark made by the shot to the inside edge of the stopboard nearest the athlete as shown in figure 4.6. The put should be measured along an extended radius of the circle. The measurement should be recorded to the nearest centimeter or quarter of an inch, whichever is closest.

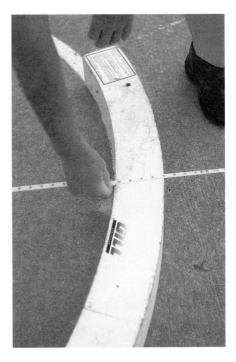

FIGURE 4.6   Measuring a put shot.

Javelin Judges

As is true of other judges in the field events, the javelin judge evaluates athletes for legal performances and measures legal throws. Three judges and two assistants officiate the event (see figure 4.7), dividing the responsibilities this way:

- *Judge 1*. Rules on all trials, records each measurement, calls out the throwing order, rules on runway violations.
- *Judge 2*. Responds to the command by judge 1 to "mark" by conducting measurements, enforces the time limit, helps rule on runway violations.

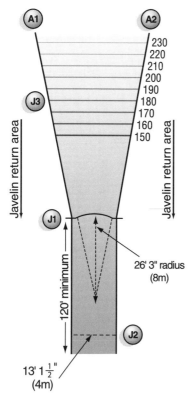

FIGURE 4.7 Positioning of javelin judges and assistants.

- *Judge 3.* Determines impact points and conducts measurements with judge 2.

- *Assistants.* Help determine impact points and carry javelins outside the sector and back to the throwing area. If assistants are not helping mark the impact, they should be outside the sector lines until the implement lands.

Legal Throw

When executing their throws, javelin throwers may hold the javelin only by the whipcord grip (see figure 4.8a). They may hold the javelin at the end of the cord grip with one or more fingers and the thumb touching the javelin shaft (see figure 4.8b). Javelin throwers have some leeway in how they grip the javelin. They can hold the shaft behind the whipcord grip with their thumb and forefinger; with their thumb, forefinger and middle finger; or with their forefinger and middle finger.

Throwers must make their throws from behind the foul-line arc. The javelin must fall within the sector made by extending the radii of the foul-line arc from the center of the arc (eight

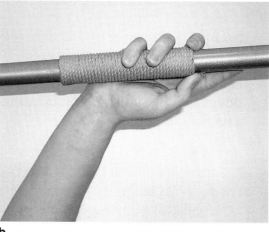

a   b

FIGURE 4.8   (*a and b*) Legal javelin grips.

meters back in the center of the runway) through the intersection of the arc with the runway lines. Throwers can't rotate through a full turn or more (i.e., 360 degrees or greater) during the approach or delivery. They must make the throw with a distinct above-the-shoulder motion of the throwing arm, as shown in figure 4.9. Their last contact with the javelin must be with the cord grip.

FIGURE 4.9   Proper throwing motion for the javelin.

Foul Throw

Javelin throwers commit a foul if they do any of the following:

- They make a 360-degree turn before the javelin is in flight.
- They use a delivery other than an over-arm, above-the-shoulder motion of the throwing arm.
- They throw the javelin so that it lands on or outside a sector line.
- They touch on or over the runway lines or on or over the foul-line arc and extensions with any part of their bodies before the judge calls, "Mark!"
- They don't hold the javelin by the whipcord grip.
- They don't exit the runway behind the foul-line arc after the javelin has landed and the judge calls, "Mark!"
- They don't initiate a trial that's completed within one minute after being called.

Measuring Throws

Javelin throws are measured from the nearest edge of the first point of contact made by the javelin to the point of the inside edge of the circumference of the arc, in line with the center of the circle behind the arc (eight meters back in the center of the runway) as shown in figure 4.10. Measurements should be to the nearest lesser inch or even-numbered centimeter.

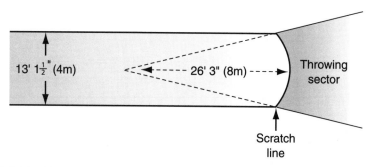

FIGURE 4.10   Proper measurement for the javelin event.

High-Jump Judges

Four high-jump judges officiate the high-jump event (see figure 4.11). The judges rule on legal and illegal jumps and do the jump measurements. The games committee specifies what marking material, if any, the athletes

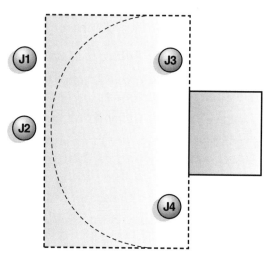

FIGURE 4.11   The high-jump area and positioning of judges.

can use for marking their takeoff points, as well as the number, location and method for placing the marks.

The responsibilities of the four judges are divided this way:

- *Judge 1.* Observes the takeoff area, rules on all trials, measures each height, calls the jumping order, marks the legal placement of the standards.
- *Judge 2.* Enforces the time limit and controls the jumping area.
- *Judges 3 and 4.* Determine contact with the crossbar, look for fouls and retrieve and replace the crossbar.

Legal Jumps and Failed Attempts

In a legal high jump the athlete jumps from one foot. A failed attempt occurs if any of the following happen:

- The jumper displaces the crossbar in an attempt to clear it.
- The jumper touches the ground or landing area beyond the plane of the crossbar with any part of his or her body or touches the crossbar extended without clearing the bar.
- After clearing the bar, the jumper contacts the upright and displaces the crossbar or steadies the bar.
- The jumper doesn't initiate a completed attempt within one minute of being called.
- Not all of the jumper's body makes it over the bar.
- The jumper takes his or her final step with both feet.

Improperly Fastened Supports

If improperly fastened supports slip down when a jumper hits the crossbar without displacing it, the head high-jump judge should rule "no jump" and allow the jumper another trial. If the jumper has displaced the bar, the jump is a failed attempt. The standards base shouldn't be moved during competition; however, the landing pit may be adjusted if doing so doesn't delay the competition.

Measuring Jumps

High jumps are measured to the nearest lesser quarter-inch or centimeter, from a point on the same level as the takeoff to the lowest point on the upper side of the crossbar. The lowest point is typically in the center of the crossbar. The crossbar and base of the standards should be marked to ensure consistent placement of the crossbar. A displaced crossbar should be replaced on the standards in exactly the same position as before its displacement. To ensure this is done, one face of the bar should be marked for identification (figure 4.12).

FIGURE 4.12   Proper marking of the crossbars and base for high jump.

Pole-Vault Judges

Four judges and two assistants officiate the pole-vault event (figure 4.13). The focus is on conducting a safe and fair competition. All judges should know how to minimize risk during the vault. Judges also ensure that jumping aids used by athletes are legal, place the crossbar on the standards properly, judge whether jump attempts are legal and successful, and measure successful vaults.

The responsibilities of the four judges and two assistants are divided this way:

- *Judge 1.* Observes takeoff area, rules on all trials, measures each height, calls the jumping order.
- *Judge 2.* Determines contact with the crossbar and observes hands.
- *Judge 3.* Enforces the time limit and controls the runway area.
- *Judge 4.* Catches poles and determines contact with the crossbar.
- *Assistants.* Retrieve and replace the crossbar.

To help you prepare for and conduct the pole-vault event, you'll find two forms in appendix A—"Pole-Vault Event" on page 140 and "Pole-Vault Facility Checklist" on page 142.

Jumping Aids

Pole vaulters aren't allowed to place marks or markers on the runway, but they may place markers adjacent to the runway. As an aid to competitors in checking their takeoff points, meet management may provide checkmarks not more than three inches long on the runway. Vaulters may legally have marks at the distances (in feet) shown along the planting box in figure 4.14. Starting at the back of the box, mark intervals in the following manner: 6, 7, 8, 9, 10, 11, 12, 13, 20, 30, 40, 50, 60, 70, 80, 90, 100, 110 and 120 (all in feet). These marks help vaulters know at which point to begin their takeoff.

Vaulters may not wear gloves, and they may not tape their hands or fingers unless they need to protect an open wound. Vaulters *are* allowed to use chalk, an adhesive or a similar substance, such as rosin, on their hands.

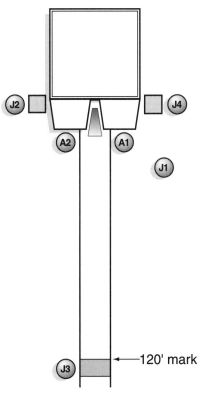

FIGURE 4.13   Vault area and positioning of the judges and assistants.

Failed Attempt

If pole vaulters do any of the following, their vault is considered a failed attempt and counts as an unsuccessful trial:

- They displace the crossbar from the pins on which it originally rested, with their bodies or poles, causing the bar to fall.
- They leave the ground but fail to clear the crossbar.
- They raise their upper hand while they're airborne to a higher point on the pole, or they raise the lower hand above the upper hand.
- They touch any part of their bodies or poles to the ground or the landing pad beyond the vertical plane of the top of the planting box without clearing the bar.
- They don't initiate a completed trial within 1-½ minutes after being called and after the crossbar and standards have been set.

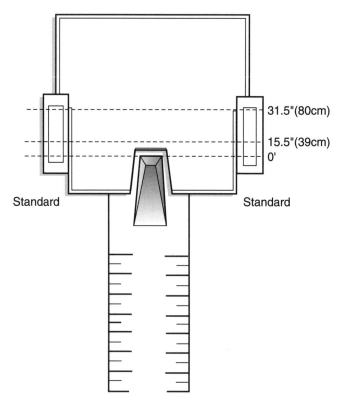

31.5"(80cm)

15.5"(39cm)

0'

Standard   Standard

FIGURE 4.14   Proper position of the crossbar and checkmarks in the pole-vault event.

- After clearing the crossbar, they contact an upright and displace the crossbar.
- They steady the crossbar with a hand or arm.
- They grip the pole above the top hand band.

If a vaulter's pole breaks during an attempt to clear the bar, the vault is redone with no penalty. No one can touch the pole during a vault unless it's falling back and away from the crossbar. However, if there's a tailwind that might cause a properly released pole to fall forward, the referee should authorize someone to catch the pole after the athlete has properly released it.

Any vaulter who uses a pole during warm-up or competition that's either improperly marked or rated below the competitor's weight (according to the manufacturer's pole rating) should be disqualified from competition. Athletes may not use training poles or variable weight poles in either warm-up or competition.

Placement of Crossbar and Checkmarks

Set the standards or uprights to position the crossbar from 15.5 inches (39 cm) beyond the vertical plane of the top of the stopboard up to a maximum of 31.5 inches (80 cm) in the direction of the landing surface as shown in figure 4.14. If improperly fastened supports slip down when a vaulter hits the crossbar without displacing it, the head vault judge rules "no vault" and allows the vaulter another trial. Should the vaulter displace the bar, however, the vault counts as a failed attempt.

Measuring Vaults

A vault's height is measured to the nearest lesser quarter-inch or centimeter. The official height is from a point on the same level as the takeoff to the lowest point on the upper side of the crossbar.

Long-Jump and Triple-Jump Judges

Four judges and two assistants conduct the long-jump and triple-jump events (figure 4.15). A wind gauge operator is involved as well (the duties of the wind gauge operator are described later in the chapter).

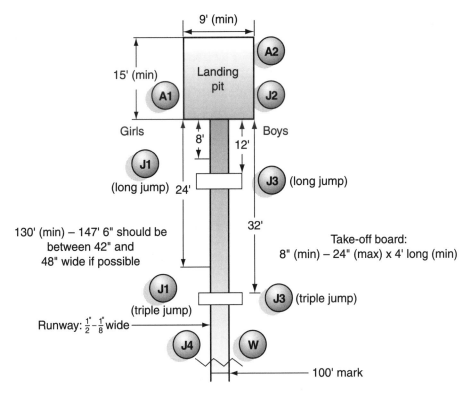

FIGURE 4.15   The jump area and positioning of the judges and assistants for the long-jump event.

The primary duties of the long-jump or triple-jump judge are assessing whether jumps are legal and measuring legal jumps. Judges use a red flag to indicate a foul and a white flag to indicate a legal jump.

The responsibilities of the judges and assistants are typically divided this way:

- *Judge 1 (the head event judge).* Rules on all trials, reads measurements, records the distances.
- *Judge 2.* Marks attempts and supervises the action around the landing pit.
- *Judge 3.* Pulls tape.
- *Judge 4 (the flight coordinator).* Calls the jumping order and enforces the time limit.
- *Assistants 1 and 2.* Level the pit.

When more than one takeoff board is available, jumpers must indicate prior to the jump which takeoff board they'll use. Jumpers may not place markers in the landing pit or runway, but they may place them alongside the runway. Only meet management may allow placement of markers alongside the landing pit.

The games committee may specify the time to open the competitive area and specify when jumpers can take their preliminary jumps, though these jumps must be taken with an official or an adult coach at the site. Competitors who don't complete all their preliminary attempts within the time specified forfeit any remaining preliminary jumps.

Legal and Foul Jumps

Jumpers must take off from behind the foul line or the foul-line extended. In the triple jump, jumpers must first land on the same foot from which they took off. In the step, they must land on the other foot from which they made their jump.

Unsuccessful trials occur when jumpers do any of the following:

- Allow a shoe to extend over the foul line or to make a mark in front of the foul line on the takeoff.
- Run across the foul line or foul-line extended.
- Fail to keep their heads in the superior position (i.e., no somersaulting).
- During the triple jump's hop phase, they fail to land on the same foot used in takeoff; in the triple jump's step phase, they don't land on the other foot from which they took off to perform the jump.

Event Guidelines

For field events there are different responsibilities depending on whether you're officiating a throwing or jumping event. These guidelines are:

Throwing Events

Cordon off the discus, shot put and javelin competition areas with rope, a fence or flags placed well outside the sector lines to help ensure the safety of spectators and athletes.

The games committee may elect to open the competitive areas and specify times for athletes to take preliminary trials (again, these trials must be taken with an official or an adult coach present). Athletes who don't complete their preliminary attempts within the time specified forfeit any remaining preliminary trials.

Athletes may not tape any part of their throwing hands or fingers unless they're protecting an open cut or wound. They may tape their wrists or wear support belts, but no gloves are allowed. To obtain a better grip, they may use chalk, an adhesive or a similar substance, such as rosin, on their hands.

When measuring a legal attempt, a nonstretchable tape (fiberglass, nylon or steel) or certified scientific measuring device, such as a laser, should be used. The tape should be held so the readings are at the end nearest the athlete; this way the athlete can immediately obtain his or her results. Don't measure a foul attempt, but do count it as a trial.

Jumping Events

In all events (high jump, pole vault, long jump and triple jump), measure only legal attempts, using nonstretchable tape (fiberglass, nylon or steel) or a certified scientific measuring device. In the high jump and pole vault, you may also use a measuring bar.

The following two procedures apply to vertical jumps only:

- The games committee determines the starting height of the bar and each successive height. When only one jumper remains in the competition, he or she may determine the next height.
- An athlete who has passed three consecutive heights after competition has begun may be permitted one warm-up without the crossbar in place. The athlete must then enter the competition at that height. Such a warm-up must occur at a height change.

- Touch the ground outside the landing pit nearer the foul line than the nearest mark made in the landing pit (while landing or leaving the pit).
- Fail to initiate a completed trial within one minute after being called.

An unsuccessful trial isn't measured but should be charged against the athlete. Note that if a jumper's trail leg touches the ground in the triple jump, this is not a violation.

Measuring Jumps

Each legal jump should be measured perpendicular to the foul line or its extension and from that point in the pit touched by the jumper or his or her apparel closest to the foul line. Measure jumps to the nearest lesser quarter-inch or centimeter. Hold the tape so the readings will be at the takeoff board—this lets jumpers know their results as soon as possible. Ideally, use a performance board so jumpers can easily see where they stand in the competition.

Wind Gauge Operator

As in some of the dashes, anemometer readings are used in the long and triple jumps to measure wind velocity so that record performances can be validated. The wind gauge operator should have a schedule of events so he or she knows the timing of the long and triple jumps. The operator positions 20 meters before the foul line and measures from the beginning of the approach to the end of the jump. The wind gauge should be placed within two meters of the runway and 1.22 meters (4 feet) high.

Wind recordings are necessary only to measure the speed of wind blowing in the direction of the jumpers—that is, a wind that aids performances. The maximum allowable average wind velocity is 4.473 miles per hour (2 meters per second). Place the anemometer facing the jumpers to measure any favoring wind. Record readings following each legal jump.

Breaking Ties

Ties often occur in field events (e.g., two long-jumpers leap the same distance or a pair of pole vaulters reach the same height). We'll now describe the procedures for breaking ties. We'll look first at how to break ties for distance in the shot put, javelin, discus, long jump and triple jump; then we'll explain how to break ties for height in the high jump or pole vault.

Breaking Distance Ties

If the distance resulting from the best performance of athletes is identical, award the higher place to the competitor whose second-best performance is better. If the tie still remains, award the higher place to the competitor whose third-best performance is better than the third-best performance of any tied competitor. Continue in this fashion until all ties are broken.

Breaking Height Ties

If athletes high jump or pole vault the same height, award the higher place to the athlete with the fewest number of trials for the last height successfully cleared. If the tie still remains, award the higher place to the athlete with the fewest total number of unsuccessful trials throughout the entire competition, up to and including the height last cleared. Passed trials don't count as misses.

If a tie still remains, and if the tie affects first place, the tied athletes make one more attempt at the height at which they failed. If no decision is reached, place the bar one inch lower in the high jump and three inches lower in the pole vault—unless the tied athletes didn't attempt the same last height (because one or more of the tied athletes passed the height). In this case, lower the bar to the lowest height last attempted by any of the remaining competitors to begin the jump-off.

If two or more of the tying contestants clear the jump-off height, raise the bar by intervals of one inch in the high jump and three inches in the pole vault. Each athlete gets one trial at each height until a winner is determined. Athletes can't pass any heights in a jump-off. Credit athletes with their best achievements in the event even if they occur in a jump-off for first place.

If the tie concerns any place other than first, award the athletes the same place, with points divided equally. If multiple athletes tie for any scoring places, add the points for the tied places and divide them equally among the tied athletes. Prior to the meet, the games committee determines if ties must be broken for purposes of advancing.

This chapter, along with the *NFHS Track and Field and Cross Country Rules Book*, should provide a good primer for administering the field events of a track and field meet. In the next chapter we'll consider what's involved in administering cross country meets.

CHAPTER 5

CROSS COUNTRY MEETS

In chapters 1 and 2 we introduced you to the purpose and philosophy of officiating cross country meets and to the responsibilities of the various officials involved in a meet: the referee and starter, the chute director, checkers, finish-line officials, timers and so on. In this chapter we'll explore the finer details of administering and officiating a cross country meet, including course preparation, flag designations, finish chutes and starting procedures.

The meet director is the person ultimately responsible for the meet's scheduling and preparation. Among many duties, the primary responsibilities of a meet director include arranging for the site, selecting and assigning officials, arranging for medical services (see "Race Administration Aids") and preparing the course for the meet. For a complete checklist of a meet director's responsibilities, see "Cross Country Meet Director Checklist" in appendix A on page 143.

A typical cross country official isn't a meet director, but what the meet director does to prepare for a meet often affects the cross country official, sometimes directly and sometimes indirectly, so the cross country official should understand the meet director's responsibilities.

Course Preparation

As mentioned, one of the meet director's responsibilities is preparing the course. Setting up proper course markers is a high priority. The director should ensure the course is marked by signs or flags placed at least 6 feet above the ground and clearly visible for 100 feet as runners approach. To mark turns, white directional lines should be drawn on the ground with chalk or paint (make sure the substance is safe for the eyes and skin). If a facility doesn't allow the use of chalk or paint, flags should be placed in the ground to mark turns.

The course should be at least three feet wide at its narrowest place. Ensure there are no ground obstructions that might trip runners or cause turned ankles. The course should also be free of overhead objects, such as tree branches, lower than eight feet above the ground.

Race Administration Aids

When a course is properly prepared and enough knowledgeable officials are in place, a cross country meet is likely to be well administered. Let's look at some factors that help to ensure the race goes well and the runners are adequately cared for:

- *First aid station.* The meet director should ensure that a readily visible and accessible first aid station is available to all athletes. If possible, the services of a doctor and trainer should be available on site.
- *Drink stations.* Drinks should be available near the finish line and, if prudent, along the race course as well. If drinks are made available along the course, assign volunteers to offer drinks to runners. Make sure the drink tables are clearly visible to the runners from a distance of 100 feet and out of the way of the course so that runners don't have to veer around the tables or other runners slowing down to get a drink.
- *Printing timer.* A timing device to record and print individual times makes tabulation of results much easier. At larger meets, more sophisticated timing systems, such as fully automatic timing (FAT) or computer chips, are often used.

The beginning of the course should include a two-inch-wide starting line and a lengthy straightaway, wide enough to accommodate everyone. Multiply the number of teams by six to arrive at the appropriate width in feet. For example, if six teams are entered, the starting line should be at least 36 feet wide.

The end of the course should have a straightaway of at least 150 yards, ending in a rope funnel with a mouth 15 feet wide. The finish line should be at the mouth of the funnel, about 15 to 25 feet from the chute. The funnel should narrow to a rope chute about 30 inches wide and at least 100 feet long (see figure 5.1). Ensure the ropes on the chute stakes are taut and the stakes near the finish line are well padded.

For large meets, multiple chutes are recommended, as shown in figure 5.2. When multiple chutes are used, there's still just one finish line with runners directed into a specific area. A rope then divides the chute so the second wave of runners finishes on the opposite side of the chute. When needed, the rope is moved again to direct the next wave of finishers. When computer chip timing and placing is used, a chute is not necessary.

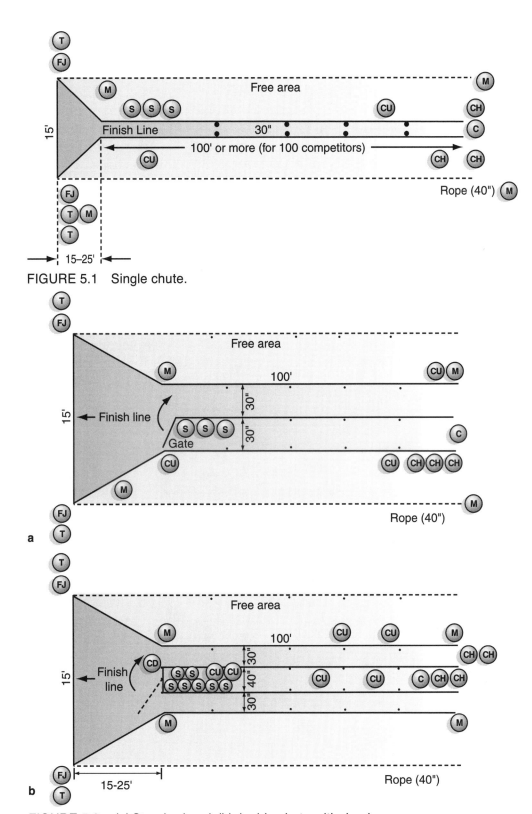

FIGURE 5.1 Single chute.

FIGURE 5.2 *(a)* Standard and *(b)* double chute with dead zone.

Starting Procedures

Cross country races are started in one of two ways: a conventional start or an audiovisual start with a countdown.

In a conventional start, the starter positions in front of the runners or off to one side, about 20 to 30 meters in front of the starting line (see figure 5.3). The starter should be easily visible to all runners and out in front enough to be able to move out of the way following the start.

Starting procedures for a conventional start are as follows:

1. Three minutes before the race begins, the starter gives all runners final instructions on course regulations, any rules clarifications and the starting and recall procedures.

2. After giving final instructions, the starter blows a loud, long blast of a whistle, or announces over the voice amp system that all runners should remove their warm-ups and prepare for the start. Run-outs aren't allowed after final instructions have been given.

3. The starter commands, "On your marks." When everyone behind the start line is motionless and steady, the starter fires the starting device.

FIGURE 5.3   Starter positioned in front of and to the side of the starting line as the race is about to start.

For an audiovisual start with a countdown, the starter positions in front of the runners, allowing enough room to move out of the way following the start. The starter should be in a spot from which he or she can observe the field of runners for the first 100 meters of the race. Whistle or flag commands should be used along with the starting device, especially in races with many runners. Figure 5.4 shows flag signals for starting a race—and for recalling it, if necessary. Assistant starters, if present, should locate where they can best observe the starting line and have a clear view of the field of runners over the first 100 meters (in case a runner falls, which might require restarting the race).

Following are the procedures for starting a race using an audiovisual start with a countdown:

1. Meet announcer calls, "Fifteen minutes to race time!" loudly enough for all runners and coaches to hear. Teams and individuals are often introduced at this point.

2. Meet announcer calls, "Three minutes to race time!" Any run-outs should have been taken by this time. Final instructions are given regarding the course, rules and starting procedures. Runners remove their warm-ups at their own discretion. It's their responsibility to be ready, in their appropriate uniforms, for the start. Following final instructions, run-outs are no longer permitted.

3. The starter calls, "Runners to the line!" Runners then line up two steps behind the starting line, or on the dashed line behind the starting line, and prepare for audiovisual signals from the starter.

4. The starter holds the starting device and red flag parallel to the ground and gives one long blast of the whistle (figure 5.4a). This is the signal for the runners to step up to the starting line, toes behind the line, and become motionless.

5. The starter slowly raises the starting device and red flag overhead (figure 5.4b). When all runners are set and motionless, and the recall starter has signaled with a white flag or hand signal that he or she approves of the position of the runners, the starter fires the starting device and, at the same time, motions downward with the red flag (figure 5.4c).

6. The starter and recall starter should observe the runners for the first 100 meters to detect any infractions and a possible need for a restart. In the case of a restart, the starter or recall starter fires the recall device and waves a white flag up and down.

Now that we've covered the responsibilities of officials in conducting track and field and cross country meets, let's move on to consider situations that might arise and see how well you can apply the rules.

a

b

c

FIGURE 5.4   *(a-c)* Starter flag signals.

PART III

APPLYING THE RULES

CHAPTER 6

PROCEDURES, CONDUCT AND COMPETITORS

As you know from the *NFHS Track and Field and Cross Country Rules Book*, there are 10 main categories of rules:

- Rule 1: Order of Events
- Rule 2: Uncontested Events and Scoring
- Rule 3: Meet Officials and Their Duties
- Rule 4: Competitors and Their Duties
- Rule 5: Running Events
- Rule 6: Throwing Events
- Rule 7: Jumping Events
- Rule 8: Special Events
- Rule 9: Cross Country
- Rule 10: Records

Note: There are no cases for Rule 8 because special events are designated by the host school with approval from the state association. However, do take a look at appendix B on page 144; this appendix is a conversion chart for scoring multiple events, which aren't offered in every state but are at the discretion of each state's association.

In the next three chapters, we'll present several cases and provide the correct rulings at the end of the chapter. Our references to the rules are meant to supplement your close study of the rules book and help bring to life some of the situations you'll face, but by no means are they meant to replace thorough study of the rules book. Before reading chapters 6 through 8, you should be well versed in all the rules as spelled out in the current *NFHS Track and Field and Cross Country Rules Book.* If you are, these chapters will help you review and test your understanding of the rules.

In this chapter, we'll consider cases in the first four rules:

- Rule 1: Order of Events
- Rule 2: Uncontested Events and Scoring
- Rule 3: Meet Officials and Their Duties
- Rule 4: Competitors and Their Duties

Rule 1: Order of Events

Rule 1 actually contains two rulings: (1) how a track team is defined (that is, which individuals are considered to be team members) and (2) how heats in races can be combined. We'll present two scenarios as well as rulings related to them. Consider how you'd respond to each situation and then check your response against the answers beginning on page 104 at the end of the chapter.

Athletes cannot be moved to another heat unless specific and carefully evaluated circumstances warrant it.

CASE 1: Unsporting Behavior

During a conference meet, an umpire observes the manager and student trainer from Pittsfield directing profanities toward athletes from other teams who are competing in the distance medley. The runners don't appear to be paying any attention to the insults. The umpire reports this to you, the referee. What do you do?

CASE 2: Girl Running in a Boys' Division

Kelli Mandrake is one of your state's best 800-meter runners; she has the second-fastest time in the state. During an invitational meet that offers a boys' and a girls' division, Mandrake requests to compete in the boys' 800 meters. Her coach thinks this will be of more value to her because the girls' division doesn't offer Mandrake much competition. There are no other factors involved; the weather is fine, and the meet will conclude well before darkness sets in. Do you allow Mandrake to run in the boys' division?

Rule 2: Uncontested Events and Scoring

Rule 2 covers event and scoring situations, such as whether an event site is acceptable or not, what to do in the case of an uncontested event, how to correct clerical and team scoring errors and what to do when you discover an ineligible athlete has participated in a meet. Consider how you'd rule in the following cases and then check your answers against the responses beginning on page 105 at the end of the chapter.

CASE 3: Hazardous Event Site
You're the referee for a triangular meet involving Jamestown, York and Brownsburg. Shortly after you arrive at the meet site, hosted by Brownsburg, you're alerted to a potentially hazardous situation at the pole-vault site. As you and the head pole-vault judge inspect the pole-vault area, you observe that the landing pad is too small to meet size specifications. What do you do?

CASE 4: High-Jump Options
Centralia is hosting an invitational meet to which five other teams have been invited. The referee has determined there's not enough padding around the high-jump pit. What should you do?

CASE 5: Scoring Error
Westwood is hosting an invitational. The meet director has mailed out an information packet to all participating schools before the meet, including a statement that "meet results are final when the referee signs and records the time at the conclusion of the meet." The day after the meet, the Richmond coach, in reviewing the meet results, realizes that his pole vaulter tied for second place but was listed as the third-place finisher. The point difference would have made Richmond the winner of the meet, rather than placing a close second, as was listed in the results. The Richmond coach calls the meet director to request that the error be corrected and Richmond be declared the winner of the invitational. As the meet director, what do you do?

CASE 6: Ineligible Athlete
Independence won their sectional meet 10 days ago, beating second-place Jamestown by two points. In the 400-meter relay, Tonya Williams anchored Independence to a win. Now meet officials discover that Williams was ineligible to participate in the meet. However, the 48-hour rule concerning scoring errors is long past. What should happen?

Rule 3: Meet Officials and Their Duties

Rule 3 covers issues involving officials and their duties. This rule defines the duties of the games committee, the use of markers, the coaching area, the appeals process, uniforms and interrupted competitions. Rule 3 also concerns when to rerun a race, when and how to disqualify athletes and what to do when a nonparticipant interferes with an event. This rule also deals with situations involving the starter, lane assignments, timing and placing and much more.

Each rule is important, but Rule 3 is of critical importance to your ability to function well as an official. The following cases are examples of some of the types of situations you'll encounter as an official. As we mentioned earlier, use these scenarios to supplement your comprehensive study of the *NFHS Track and Field and Cross Country Rules Book*. Consider how you'd respond to each situation and then check your responses against the answers beginning on page 106 at the end of the chapter.

CASE 7: Rerunning a Race?

Pittsfield is hosting a triangular meet involving Jamestown and Centralia. In the 800-meter relay, Pittsfield is disqualified for an illegal exchange, and Jamestown is disqualified because their anchor leg threw his baton in disgust after losing a close battle with Centralia's anchor. You're the meet referee. An official calls to your attention that the race was started from the wrong staggered starting lines. What do you do?

CASE 8: Notifying a Coach of Disqualification

In an invitational meet, Westwood wins their heat in the 400-meter relay race. Following the heat, the head umpire reports to you, the referee, that Westwood completed their second exchange outside of the exchange zone. You disqualify Westwood from that event and tell the head umpire to notify Westwood's coach of the situation and your decision.

However, the head umpire can't find the Westwood coach, and she's pulled away by other duties before she can notify him. The Westwood 400-meter relay team reports to the finals of the event, unaware their relay team has been disqualified. The head umpire then informs the Westwood runners that their 400-meter relay team has been disqualified because of the exchange-zone infraction committed in their heat.

At this point the Westwood coach *is* found; he appeals the decision, telling the referee that he'd not been notified of the disqualification and that, had he been notified, he would have changed the makeup of his team's 800-meter relay. His anchor runner on the 400-meter relay was listed only as an alternate on the 800-meter relay because he didn't want to tire his runner out and was saving her for the 400-meter relay finals. Had he known his runner would not be running the 400-meter relay finals, he would have used her in the 800-meter relay finals. Thus, by not being notified of the disqualification, the coach says he was put at a disadvantage in the 800-meter relay.

What is the correct ruling here? Is the Westwood coach's appeal approved or denied?

CASE 9: Close Finish

In a dual meet between York and Richmond, the boys' 400-meter dash is closely contested. The judges assigned to pick first place declare Johnny Graham, from York, the winner; however, the judges picking second place assign Graham that place. They believe that Theotis Hughes, a Richmond runner, won the race. Two of the timers say they had Graham as the winner, whereas the other first-place timer says he had Hughes as the winner. Who should be declared the winner?

CASE 10: Reporting Interference

In the girls' 800-meter run of a sectional meet, an alleged violation of runner interference is reported to you, the referee, by one of the finish-line judges. However, the umpire assigned to the area in which the alleged violation occurred reported no interference. How do you rule?

Would your ruling be any different if the alleged violation was reported by two members of the jury of appeals, who are sitting in the stands? Or by an umpire stationed on the opposite side of the track from where the alleged violation occurred?

Rule 4: Competitors and Their Duties

Rule 4 covers a broad range of situations concerning competitors and competition, including entry, participation and advancement rules; uniform and shoe regulations; athletes' behavior; interference rules; official starts and finishes of an event; coaching athletes during competitions; and much more. Study the *NFHS Track and Field and Cross Country Rules Book* diligently so you'll know how to respond to the great variety of situations that arise in a meet. Here, test your knowledge in a sampling of the situations covered by Rule 4. Consider how you'd rule in the following cases and then check your answers against the answers beginning on page 107 at the end of the chapter.

CASE 11: Arriving Late to the Event

In a triangular meet held at Jamestown, the Brownsburg team arrives late because of transportation problems. By the time the Brownsburg athletes pile off the bus, the field events have already begun. Mike Chadsworth, a Brownsburg shot putter, reports to his event after the first round of trials has been completed. Is he allowed to compete?

What if Chadsworth reported after all the preliminary trials had been completed? Would your ruling be different?

Similarly, what about a Brownsburg high-jumper who reports late to his event, which began at 5 feet, 10 inches, and after the first-round trials have been completed, the bar is now at 6 feet? Can the Brownsburg high-jumper enter the competition?

CASE 12: Participating in Too Many Events?

Deanna Sandler, an athlete from Pittsfield, is entered in three individual events (the 100 meters, 200 meters and 400 meters) and two relays (the 400-meter and 1,600-meter relays). After Sandler has completed all the events, meet management realizes she has participated in five events. As referee, what should you do?

CASE 13: Unacceptable Conduct?

Michael Tarry, a sprinter from York, is favored to win the 100-meter race in his conference. He's also expected to do well in the 200 meters and two other events. He makes it easily to the finals of the 100-meter race, but in the race he pulls up slightly lame near the end and finishes second to a rival he has beaten several times during the year. In frustration, Tarry utters a profanity, not directed at anyone. The head finish judge hears the profanity and reports the infraction to you, the referee. What is your ruling?

CASE 14: Runner Interference?

In the 1,600-meter run of a dual meet between Centralia and Westwood, Anita Simmons of Centralia leads Jessie Hall of Westwood. As they come around the final curve, Simmons veers away from the curb and into the path of Hall, who breaks stride momentarily to keep from bumping into Simmons and then changes direction, trying to pass Simmons on the inside. Simmons, however, changes direction to stay in the path of Hall, and Hall is unable to pass Simmons. No contact is ever made between the two runners. What call, if any, should be made in this situation?

Answers

The correct answers to the scenarios presented in this chapter are provided here. Compare your responses to see which areas you might need to review.

Case 1: Unsporting Behavior

An inexperienced referee might be tempted to ignore the situation because it appeared to have no effect on the race, and perhaps because the profanities were coming not from athletes or coaches but from other team personnel. However, neither of these factors should affect your ruling. You should disqualify the Pittsfield manager and student trainer from the meet for unsporting behavior and disqualify the Pittsfield distance medley team from the event. Managers and trainers are as much a part of a team as athletes and coaches are, and when team members act inappropriately, the team should be penalized.

Case 2: Girl Running in a Boys' Division

No, you don't allow Kelli Mandrake to run in the boys' 800 meters. It's true that the games committee can decide to combine boys' and girls' heats and score them separately, if the head coaches all agree to this (for instance, if you need to get the races in before dark). But an individual athlete can't be moved from one heat or division to another simply because she wants to. This rule guards against athletes gaining a competitive advantage in a different heat (in this case, Mandrake, the female runner, might be pushed to a better 800-meter time because of the faster competition in another heat).

Case 3: Hazardous Event Site

First and foremost, you cancel the pole-vault competition; you can't allow the competition to take place with landing pads that don't meet specifications. As for awarding points, if you awarded no points at all or chose to split the points evenly among the three teams, either way you'd be incorrect. You should divide the 11 pole-vault points evenly to the two visiting teams—5-½ points to Jamestown and 5-½ to York. Brownsburg, the host team responsible for providing a safe pole-vault area, receives no points.

Case 4: High-Jump Options

Here is another situation in which safety must come first. When equipment specifications aren't met, you can't hold events using the equipment. In this case, all visiting teams should share the points equally, and the host team should get no points. If it's possible to borrow padding from another school and modify the event schedule so the high jump can be contested later in the meet, this is not only acceptable but desirable.

Case 5: Scoring Error

This is an unfortunate error indeed. It's always tough to lose a close meet, and it's tougher yet to do so because of a scoring error. As stated in the *NFHS Track and Field and Cross Country Rules Book*, clerical errors such as this one can be corrected if discovered and brought to the attention of the meet director within 48 hours of the meet's conclusion. However, because the games committee had established a different time for the correction of errors (that is, by the end of the meet), the error can't be corrected the following day; the final results remain as they were recorded the day before, at the end of the meet, with Richmond in second place.

Ineligibility corrections regarding meet participants can be made at any time, even for past events.

Case 6: Ineligible Athlete

Tonya Williams should be declared ineligible, as she was, and Independence should be stripped of their points in the 400-meter relay (and in any other event in which Williams scored). As a result, Jamestown would be the winner of the sectional, because the adjusted point total puts them in first place. It doesn't matter how long after the meet that the error is discovered; an ineligible athlete can't score points for her team. Corrections made necessary because of an ineligible athlete may be made at any time.

Case 7: Rerunning a Race?

When rerunning a race, only contestants eligible to run may participate. Because Pittsfield and Jamestown were disqualified from the race, they're ineligible to participate in a rerun. So, you have two choices here—you can rerun the race and allow only Centralia to run, or you can simply declare Centralia the winner of the race. If the race is not rerun, Centralia won't have an official winning time, but a winning time is not necessary for a team to be declared the winner. If an official time isn't needed for qualifying, placing or record purposes, it makes more sense simply to declare the winner without rerunning the race.

Case 8: Notifying a Coach of Disqualification

You should deny the Westwood coach's appeal. The head umpire was in error in not informing the coach or the Westwood 400-meter relay runners of the disqualification immediately after you made the ruling, but that doesn't negate the disqualification. The head umpire should have informed the Westwood runners while they were still in the finish-line area following their heat that an infraction had been reported and a ruling would be made soon. When the head umpire could not immediately locate the Westwood coach to inform her of the disqualification, the umpire should have had the public address announcer announce the disqualification. Regardless, the disqualification stands.

Case 9: Close Finish

Graham, the runner from York, is the winner. The decision of judges picking the higher place overrules the decision of judges selecting a lower place. The matter doesn't concern the timers at all; timers should time the race and leave the finish order to the finish judges.

Case 10: Reporting Interference

It is not the finish-line judge's responsibility to serve as an umpire and call violations. As long as an umpire didn't report a violation, and you, as the referee, didn't observe a violation, you shouldn't disqualify the runner. The same goes for when two members of the jury of appeals report a violation in this situation. If another umpire reports the violation (in this case one on the opposite side of the track from where the alleged violation took place), make your decision based on the information you receive from the head umpire. You should always give great consideration to the reports of the umpires in the area in which any alleged violation occurred.

Case 11: Arriving Late to the Event

You should allow the Brownsburg shot putter to enter the competition after the first round of trials. However, if all preliminary trials have been completed, and the qualifiers are already determined, it's too late for him to enter the competition. In the case of the high-jumper, you should allow him to enter the competition at the current height of 6 feet.

Ordinarily, you should strictly enforce entry deadlines, but in dual and triangular meets in which entries are made when the event is called, you have some leeway if circumstances warrant, as they do in this case. Apply preventive officiating and common sense when athletes are delayed entry because of circumstances beyond their control.

Case 12: Participating in Too Many Events?

Deanna Sandler has violated the rule regarding participation limitations by competing in five events. Thus, she is disqualified; you should take away any places and points she earned in any of her events, so, in the case of the two relays she ran, her team is disqualified from those events.

Note that it wouldn't matter if Sandler participated in the relays only in preliminary heats and not the finals; she still competed in the events. An athlete is considered to have competed in an event when he or she reports to the clerk of the course or the judge of a field event in which he or she is entered.

Case 13: Unacceptable Conduct?

You should disqualify Michael Tarry from the 100 meters for unacceptable behavior, thus not awarding his team the points he would have earned for finishing second. However, this is *not* a case of unsporting behavior, which would have called for Tarry's disqualification from the entire meet. Had he directed his profanity at an official, an athlete or anyone else, his actions would have constituted unsporting behavior. As it was, his behavior is not acceptable and results in disqualification from the event.

Case 14: Runner Interference?

Contact doesn't have to be made for interference to occur. Interference occurred when Simmons caused Hall to break stride. Even if Hall hadn't had to break stride, you should still call interference and disqualify Simmons because she tried to block Hall from legally passing her.

CHAPTER 7

Track & Field Events

In chapter 6 we looked at situations concerning procedures, conduct and competitors that you might face as an official—that is, situations related to the first four rules in the *NFHS Track and Field and Cross Country Rules Book*. In this chapter we'll look at the next three rules:

- Rule 5: Running Events
- Rule 6: Throwing Events
- Rule 7: Jumping Events

As you did in chapter 6, read through each case and decide how you would respond. Then check your answers at the end of the chapter.

Rule 5: Running Events

As you might imagine, this rule covers a lot of territory, addressing issues pertaining to alleys, equipment use, qualifying procedures, running races in sections, lane assignments, starting devices, fallen runners and recalled races, relay entries and substitutions, baton exchanges and much more. The following cases offer glimpses into some of the kinds of situations you might run into as an official for running events; be sure to study the *NFHS Track and Field and Cross Country Rules Book* to thoroughly acquaint yourself with the myriad of rules that govern the running of races. Consider how you'd respond to each situation and then check your answers against the answers beginning on page 114 at the end of the chapter.

CASE 1: Qualifying for the Finals
In a conference meet involving several teams on an eight-lane track, including a team from Jamestown, meet management announces that three semifinal heats will be run, with the first two finishers in each heat, plus the two fastest third-place finishers, advancing to the finals. Following the semifinals of the 100-meter dash, meet officials determine that the two fastest third-place runners were in heats one and two.

However, the Jamestown coach appeals, pointing out the Jamestown runner who placed fourth in heat one had a faster time than the third-place finisher in heat two. Because her runner had the faster time, the Jamestown coach argues that she should advance to the finals. What should happen in this case?

CASE 2: False Start

You're the starter for the 100-meter race in a triangular meet between Pittsfield, York and Brownsburg. A Pittsfield runner breaks from the starting line after you've given the set command but before you fire the starting device. A runner from York and one from Brownsburg follow the Pittsfield runner out of the blocks. Are all three runners disqualified for false starts, or is only the Pittsfield runner disqualified?

CASE 3: To Restart or Not to Restart

In a dual meet between Centralia and Westwood, a curved starting line is used for the girls' 3,200-meter run. One of the runners for Westwood

For races run in heats, the rules support the idea that place is more important than time and advancement will be dependent on this.

is inadvertently bumped by another runner and falls as she attempts to move, on the first turn, toward the inside lane. Should the race be restarted?

What if the Westwood runner's fall was not caused by contact with another runner but she simply fell without touching anyone else? Would your ruling be different?

CASE 4: Retrieving a Baton

During the 1,600-meter relay, the anchor leg for the Richmond team drops the baton while outside and beyond the exchange zone. Can he pick it up and continue the race?

Would your ruling be different if he dropped the baton within the exchange zone, where he picked it up? What if he dropped the baton within the exchange zone and the baton rolled into an adjacent lane, where he picked it up? Is this legal?

Rule 6: Throwing Events

Rule 6 focuses on aspects of throwing events, including trials, tie-breaking procedures, unsporting conduct, equipment specifications and situations that concern the specific events. Consider how you'd rule in the following cases and then check your answers against the responses beginning on page 115 at the end of the chapter.

CASE 5: Tie-Breaking Situation?

In a conference meet, shot putters from Independence and Jamestown tie with their longest marks for the last qualifying spot to advance to the finals. The shot-put judge advances the Independence athlete to the finals because his second-longest put was longer than the Jamestown athlete's second-longest put. Do you agree with this ruling?

CASE 6: Legal Throw?

After completing her discus throw, an athlete from Centralia stays under control within the ring until her discus lands. The judge calls ,"Mark!" After the call, the thrower exits at the front of the ring. The judge raises his red flag and calls out, "Do not measure!" The Centralia coach appeals to the field referee, claiming that the judge declared the throw legal when he said, "Mark." What's the call?

CASE 7: Legal Put?

Before his put, a Richmond shot putter takes position in the back of the ring, pauses, shifts the shot several times between his right and left hand, and then, as he shifts the shot to his putting hand on his final shift, immediately begins his glide across the circle. As he moves through the circle, he holds the shot close to his chin, and his hand doesn't drop below this position during the putting action. The shot lands between the sector lines, the event judge calls, "Mark!" and the shot putter exits through the back half of the circle. Is his attempt legal?

CASE 8: Measuring a Javelin Throw

A javelin thrower from Independence makes a throw that lands with the point touching just prior to the rest of the javelin, which slides along the ground on the shaft. How should you measure this throw?

What if the javelin touches down almost flat but with the rear portion of the shaft touching just before the rest of the javelin, which then slides along the ground—how would you measure this throw? What if the javelin were to touch with the shaft perfectly flat?

Rule 7: Jumping Events

The rule for jumping events covers the order of competition, time limits, excuses to compete in other events, jump-offs, landing pad specifications, trials and many specifics within each individual event. Rule 7 is quite extensive, covering a multitude of situations you need to become familiar with. Consider how you would rule in the following situations and then check your answers against the responses beginning on page 115 at the end of the chapter.

CASE 9: Illegal Pass?

Ashley Hampton, a high-jumper from Jamestown, has taken three running approaches at the high jump but hasn't jumped yet. Realizing she won't be able to begin another approach within the one-minute time limit, Hampton yells "Pass!" to you, the event judge. Should you allow her to pass?

CASE 10: Competing in Multiple Events

Donovan Peters, an athlete from Centralia, has just made his first unsuccessful attempt at high jumping a height of 6 feet, 4 inches. As the high-jump judge, you excuse Peters to run in the first heat of the 110-meter high hurdles preliminaries. In the high hurdles, one runner interferes with another, so the referee orders the race to be rerun following the third heat.

Because of the rerun, Peters reports back to you 15 minutes after being excused, and the bar is now set at 6 feet, 6 inches. Peters did not want to pass any attempts at 6 feet, 4 inches. What do you do?

CASE 11: Changing Entry Height

Pittsfield high-jumper LaVell Edwards informs you, the high-jump judge, that he is going to pass until the bar reaches 6 feet, 6 inches. He tells you this before the competition begins. When the bar is raised to

6 feet, 4 inches, and before competition has begun at that height, Edwards requests permission to jump at that height. Do you allow him to jump?

What if Edwards asked you after competition began at 6 feet, 4 inches? What if he asked you after his flight had finished competition at 6 feet, 4 inches, but other flights were still going to jump at that height?

CASE 12: Touching the Crossbar

Westwood pole vaulter Calvin Grady clears the crossbar on an attempt, but as he goes over it, he touches the bar, causing it to bounce up. While coming down, Grady is able to steady the bar with his hand, keeping it on the pin setting. You, as the pole-vault judge, rule that this is a failed

Holding or steadying the crossbar in an attempt to keep it from falling is considered a violation and a failed attempt should be called.

attempt because Grady touched the bar in an obvious attempt to keep it up. Grady's coach appeals your decision, saying the bar was never dislodged from its original setting. Who's right, you or the coach?

Answers

The correct answers to the scenarios presented in this chapter are provided here. Compare your responses to see which areas you might need to review.

Case 1: Qualifying for the Finals

Although the third-place finisher in heat two had a slower time than the fourth-place Jamestown runner in heat one, the third-place finisher in heat two should advance to the finals. It's the games committee's right to determine who moves on, and the committee made it clear before the meet what the qualifying procedures were. The rules support the idea of place being more important than time. In races run in heats, it's more desirable to qualify on head-to-head competition than on time.

Case 2: False Start

Whether all three runners are disqualified for false starts depends on whether, in your opinion as the starter, they each, individually, committed a false start. The Pittsfield runner, the one who broke first, is definitely disqualified. The York and Brownsburg runners would be disqualified as well if you believe they jumped on their own, as opposed to reacting to the false start made by the Pittsfield runner. It's possible for more than one runner to be disqualified at the same time for a false start.

Case 3: To Restart or Not to Restart

If you observe that the Westwood runner fell after an inadvertent bump (or after interference) by another runner, the race should be recalled and restarted. In the case of interference, the runner who interfered with the Westwood runner should be disqualified. If the contact was inadvertent, no one is disqualified.

If the Westwood runner falls on her own, with no contact from another runner, the race shouldn't be recalled. The accident is unfortunate for the Westwood runner, but if it's clear no contact was made to cause the fall, the race shouldn't be recalled. If there's any doubt whether contact occurred, the race should be recalled.

Case 4: Retrieving a Baton

If the Richmond runner drops the baton while outside the exchange zone, he can pick it up and continue racing as long as he doesn't interfere with other runners. If he drops the baton within the exchange zone, and he picks it up either within the zone or in an adjacent lane, again he can continue running as long as he doesn't interfere with other runners. (In fact, his teammate can pick it up and hand it to him again, as long as the new exchange is made within the zone.) The runner must return to his assigned lane, however, before passing the limit of the exchange zone, or his team will be disqualified.

Case 5: Tie-Breaking Situation?

We hope you don't agree with this ruling, because it was made in error. Tie-breaking procedures don't apply to preliminary competitions; they apply only to finals. Both shot putters should advance to the finals.

Case 6: Legal Throw?

The throw is illegal. Yes, it *was* legal—until the Centralia athlete stepped out of the front of the ring. Anytime a thrower steps out of the front of the ring, the throw is a foul. If you're the head judge for a throwing event, take the time before the event to explain to the athletes the procedures for entering and exiting the circle.

Remember that the call of "Mark!" indicates not that a throw is legal but that the athlete can exit the circle. Under NFHS rules, the athlete must exit from the back half of the ring. An athlete stepping out of the front of the ring is an informal signal to the referee not to measure.

Case 7: Legal Put?

Yes, the Richmond shot putter's attempt is legal. As long as he paused after entering the circle, it's okay to shift the shot from one hand to the other before beginning his motion across the ring. The required pause is intended to prevent a thrower from entering the circle and immediately beginning the shift or glide across the circle in one continuous movement, thereby adding momentum to the shot not generated within the ring.

Case 8: Measuring a Javelin Throw

In the first case, with the point touching just prior to the rest of the javelin, which slides along the ground on the shaft, you should measure from the spot at which the furthermost tip of the javelin first touched the ground. If the javelin were to fall almost flat, with the rear portion touching just before the rest of the shaft touched and slid along the ground, you should measure from the point at which the rearmost part of the javelin touched down—that is, at the point of initial contact. If the shaft is perfectly flat as it touches, measure from the end of the cord grip nearest to the scratch line.

Case 9: Illegal Pass?

No, you shouldn't allow Hampton to pass to the next height in the high jump. This situation highlights a common abuse by jumpers who have either exceeded the time limit or are close to exceeding it. Athletes must declare their intent to pass when you call them for their trial or before the start of the clock to measure the allowable one minute in which they must initiate a jump that they complete. So, in this case, you should record a failed attempt for Hampton.

Case 10: Competing in Multiple Events
Peters has two trials left at the new height of 6 feet, 6 inches. When he didn't return in time to take his remaining jumps at 6 feet, 4 inches, he is considered to have passed on those trials, and he must continue in the competition along with the other jumpers at the new height.

Case 11: Changing Entry Height
Even though Edwards said he was going to enter the competition at 6 feet, 6 inches, he can change his mind, as long as he does so before the competition begins at any new height that's below 6 feet, 6 inches. So, yes he may enter at 6 feet, 4 inches, if he requests to do so before the competition at that height has begun.

He can also enter at 6 feet, 4 inches, if his flight has begun competition at that height and is still jumping at it. He would have to take his regular position in the order of trials, meaning if his turn has come and gone once at 6 feet, 4 inches, that will be counted as a missed trial. (In such a case, he would have two remaining trials at that height.)

If his flight at that height has already been completed, he can't begin competition until the next height.

Case 12: Touching the Crossbar
You're right. It's considered a failed attempt if a pole vaulter steadies the crossbar with his or her arms or hands. Touching the bar in an attempt to clear it is not necessarily a violation, but holding or steadying the bar in an attempt to keep it from falling is a violation.

CHAPTER 8

CROSS COUNTRY AND RECORDS

Some of the information in the previous two chapters applied to cross country as well as to track and field, but in part of this chapter we'll focus on cross country, exploring officiating issues directly derived from cross country meets. We'll also present situations involving record setting in track and field. The material in this chapter is based on Rule 9 (Cross Country) and Rule 10 (Records).

Rule 9: Cross Country

This rule covers topics in administering a cross country meet, including course markings, course obstructions, meets including individual entries, finishes, breaking ties, team scoring, disqualifications and more. We'll present several of the kinds of scenarios you might encounter as a cross country official. Consider how you'd rule in each situation and then check your answers against those beginning on page 120 at the end of the chapter.

CASE 1: Lines and Flags

In a dual meet between Jamestown and Pittsfield, the Pittsfield course is marked with white directional lines and with flags. The person laying out the course made an error with the white lines—at one spot the line passes on the right side of a yellow flag instead of on the left. (Runners are supposed to keep yellow flags to their right as they make a right turn after the flag.)

The lead runner in the meet, Adam Van Gleason from Jamestown, follows the directional line in that spot instead of keeping the yellow flag to his right and turning after passing the flag. He stayed directly on the line for the whole turn. The other runners kept the flag to their right as they passed it and turned right, as they were supposed to.

In races where computer chips are used, they should take priority over the picks of the finish-line judges.

Van Gleason finishes first but is disqualified for not completing the course. The Jamestown coach claims his runner followed the directional line, that the course was incorrectly laid out, and that the error was made by the person who laid out the course, not by his runner.

Should Van Gleason have been disqualified, or is his coach right?

CASE 2: Breaking Ties

In an invitational meet, York and Brownsburg tie for third place. York has six runners in the meet, and Brownsburg has five. How do you break the tie?

How would you break the tie if each team had five runners?

CASE 3: Using Computer Chips

Computer chips in shoes are being used in an invitational meet to determine the order of finish. Megan Riley of Centralia dives across the finish line in a close finish with Katy Padilla of Westwood. The judges at the finish line pick Riley ahead of Padilla, because Riley's torso crossed the line first. But when the official results are tabulated using the computer chips, Padilla has finished ahead of Riley—her shoes crossed the line before Riley's shoes. Who should get the higher place?

CASE 4: What's the Score?

In a dual meet pitting Richmond against Independence, Richmond has 5 runners and Independence has 10. Richmond's runners place 1, 2, 6, 7 and 15, whereas Independence runners place 3, 4, 5, 8, 9, 10, 11, 12, 13 and 14. The Richmond coach claims his team won 28-29; the Independence coach says *his* team won 29-31. Which coach is correct?

Rule 10: Records

Rule 10 covers various record situations, such as when a record is valid, if an athlete can set a record in an event won with a nonrecord performance, how jump-offs affect dual record-setters and so on. Consider how you'd rule in the following situations and check your answers against the responses beginning on page 121 at the end of the chapter.

CASE 5: A Record in the Prelims?

Derek Markstall of Jamestown sets a record in the discus throw in the preliminary round. However, in the finals, his best throw is not as good as his record throw in the prelims. Does his record stand?

CASE 6: Additional Trials for a Record?

Amy Blankenship, a Centralia shot putter, wins the shot put at a triangular meet. Her best put is two inches short of the school record. Immediately after the competition is concluded and the places are determined, she asks you, the shot-put judge, if she can have additional trials to attempt to set a school record. Do you allow her the additional trials?

CASE 7: Does the Record Count?

The state record in the pole vault is 15 feet, 8 inches. At the state meet, Todd Wiley of Pittsfield and Ian Allender of Westwood both clear 15 feet, 7 inches, but fail at 15 feet, 10 inches. After applying the formula to break ties, the tie remains, and a jump-off is necessary.

Both Wiley and Allender clear the bar at 15 feet, 4 inches, and again at 15 feet, 7 inches. Wiley misses at 15 feet, 10 inches, but Allender clears the bar at that height, winning the jump-off at a height 2 inches better than the state record. Allender is awarded the win, but is he also awarded the state record, seeing as the record came in a jump-off?

CASE 8: One Record Holder or Two?

In the high jump, Tisa Williams of Pittsfield and Sarah Longley of Brownsburg are tied at a record height. Williams wins the ensuing jump-off at a lower height than the record height. Are both Williams and Longley recognized as record setters, or is only the event winner, Williams, recognized as having set a new record?

Answers

The correct answers to the scenarios presented in this chapter are provided here. Compare your responses to see which areas you might need to review.

Jump-offs are considered part of the competition and state records can be set during these times.

Case 1: Lines and Flags

The officials were correct in disqualifying Van Gleason. It's an unfortunate error, and the incorrect markings should have been called to the attention of all runners before the race started, but the rules clearly state that directional flags take priority over any other course markings.

Case 2: Breaking Ties

If York had six runners complete the course and Brownsburg had five, and their score is tied, York gets the higher place. When the score is tied after comparing the first five finishers from each team, you go to the sixth-place finishers for each. If one team doesn't have a sixth runner, the team that does have six is awarded the higher place.

If York and Brownsburg tied, and each had five runners, the tie is broken by totaling the scores of the first four runners for each team.

Case 3: Using Computer Chips
Padilla gets the higher place. In races in which computer chips are used, place and time are recorded when the computer chips in the shoes cross the finish line. Computer chips take priority over the picks of finish-line judges.

Case 4: What's the Score?
The Richmond coach is correct—his team wins, 28-29. While it's true that his runners totaled 31 points, based strictly on the finish places of their five runners, a team can only have seven runners figure into the scoring. Because Independence's seventh runner finished in 11th place, the Independence runners who placed 12th, 13th and 14th don't factor into the scoring, which means the Richmond runner who placed 15th is given 12th place. This brings Richmond's total down from 31 to 28 and gives them the 1-point win.

Case 5: A Record in the Prelims?
Yes, Markstall's record stands. It doesn't matter if his best throw came in preliminary rounds or in the finals, and how he performs in later rounds makes no difference. He's simply credited with his best performance, period.

Case 6: Additional Trials for a Record?
No, you shouldn't allow her additional trials. The competition is over; she had her chances during the competition.

Case 7: Does the Record Count?
It's a banner day for Allender—he gets the win and a state record. Even though he didn't break the record before the jump-off with his opponent, he did break it during the jump-off, and that's considered part of the competition. Records can be set in jump-offs.

Case 8: One Record Holder or Two?
Both high-jumpers are recognized as record setters. They both jumped a record height in competition. It doesn't matter who wins the jump-off. Williams, of course, is awarded first place, and her team is awarded her first-place points, whereas Longley's team is given her second-place points—but both girls are recognized as sharing the record.

APPENDIX A

Checklists and Forms

This appendix contains checklists and forms that will be useful when you are officiating track and field and cross country meets. You may reproduce and use these checklists and forms as needed.

Meet Information Checklist

Meet: _____

Date: _____ Time: _____

- ❏ Date and time of meet confirmed
- ❏ Site of meet confirmed
- ❏ Confirmation that the meet is officially sanctioned
- ❏ Type of competition (dual, triangular or invitational) confirmed
- ❏ Method of confirming acceptance
- ❏ Meet schedule

- ❏ Time schedule and time limits
- ❏ Scoring system
- ❏ Number of entrants allowed
- ❏ Entry form and fees
- ❏ Qualifying standards (if applicable)
- ❏ Participation limits (if more restrictive than the *NFHS Track and Field and Cross Country Rules Book*)

- ❏ Equipment or implements to be provided
- ❏ Inspection procedure for field event implements
- ❏ Lodging, meal information, concession facilities
- ❏ Awards
- ❏ Coaches' meeting places and times
- ❏ List of premeet and postmeet activities
- ❏ Publicity data required, location of awards stand, other special instructions

- ❏ Identification of special events
- ❏ List of prohibited items and special instructions (e.g., alcoholic beverages, tobacco, radio and stereo equipment, wireless communication devices, jewelry, hats, sunglasses)
- ❏ Ticket information
- ❏ List of phone numbers for meet personnel

Description of facilities, including:

- ❏ Location of dressing rooms
- ❏ Type of running surface
- ❏ Type of approach surfaces
- ❏ Type of throwing surface and size of throwing sectors
- ❏ Length of spikes allowed
- ❏ Parking areas
- ❏ Training room or medical areas
- ❏ Seating arrangements for coaches and athletes
- ❏ Warm-up areas and restrictions

- ❏ Check-in area
- ❏ List of restrictions, if any, on marking surfaces
- ❏ Restricted areas in which coaches, athletes and spectators are not allowed
- ❏ Area of competition in which removal of the team uniform is prohibited
- ❏ Entrance gate for athletes, coaches, officials and complimentary ticket holders

Event Equipment Checklist

Meet: _____

Date: _____ Time: _____

Field Event Equipment

- ❏ Implement inspection area with scales, gauges and other equipment
- ❏ Ladders, lift or aerial bucket
- ❏ Measuring devices and watches
- ❏ Clipboards including schedule, event record, entry list, rules books, pencils
- ❏ Crossbars, standards, and pole-vault and high-jump measuring bar
- ❏ Red and white flags
- ❏ Sector boundary flags
- ❏ Brooms, shovels, rakes
- ❏ Anemometer (wind gauge) for the long jump and triple jump
- ❏ Performance indicators
- ❏ Wind sock for pole vault, long and triple jump
- ❏ Athletic tape or chalk to mark outline of standards
- ❏ Orange cones (18 inches high) to identify closed areas

Track Event Equipment

- ❏ Watches or FAT equipment
- ❏ Clipboards including schedule, entry list, rules books, pencils, event sheets, list of records, heat sheets, finish judges' and timers' cards or pads
- ❏ Yellow, white and red flags for umpires and head finish judge
- ❏ Diagram of umpires' stations
- ❏ Judges' and timers' stands
- ❏ Anemometer (wind gauge) for dashes
- ❏ Hurdles and a transport vehicle
- ❏ Cones/flags for break-line designation
- ❏ Batons
- ❏ Starting blocks and a transport vehicle
- ❏ Lane indicators
- ❏ Starter's equipment
- ❏ Hip numbers, if used with FAT

Other Equipment

- ❏ Contestant numbers, pins, tape and hip numbers, if required
- ❏ Medical and training room supplies
- ❏ PA system and portable communication items
- ❏ ID badges
- ❏ Clerk of the course sheets
- ❏ Equipment to facilitate a drawing by lot
- ❏ Extra numbers and pins
- ❏ Record application forms
- ❏ Jury of appeals forms
- ❏ Umpires' forms and infraction cards
- ❏ Tables, chairs, tents
- ❏ Awards and award stand
- ❏ Lap counter and bell
- ❏ National anthem (recorded)
- ❏ U.S. flag
- ❏ Benches for contestants
- ❏ Caps, shirts or jackets for staff
- ❏ Implement headquarters area
- ❏ Implement first aid area
- ❏ Implement press area
- ❏ Cart with baskets to transport warm-ups from starting to finish area
- ❏ Computer scoring forms
- ❏ Water for contestants and staff

From *Officiating Track & Field and Cross Country*, ASEP, 2005, Champaign, IL: Human Kinetics.

Track and Field and Cross Country Appeal Form

Contestant: _____ Number: _____

School: _____

Date and time of submission to referee: _____

Area of concern: (*circle one*)   *RUNNING EVENT*   *FIELD EVENT*

Event: _____

Rule reference: _____

Description of appeal:

Head coach signature: _____

School: _____

For referee use only:

Ruling: _____

_____

Signature: _____

Date: _____ **Time:** _____

Team Score Sheet

Places to be counted: *6*

Scoring: *10-8-6-4-2-1*

Event \ Place	1st	2nd	3rd	4th	5th	6th

Team names \ Event										Totals

High School Track and Field Record Application

National Federation of State High School Associations
PO Box 690; Indianapolis, Indiana 46206; Phone: 317-972-6900

Please type or print all requested information. The required signatures must be included on three copies of this form before sending it to your state high school association for the executive officer's signature. The state association must then forward two copies to the National Federation of State High School Associations for consideration. (*Note:* For a performance to be recognized as a national record, it shall have been made in a meet involving five or more schools.)

Date of application: _____, 20 _____

This application is submitted for an outdoor record in (event): _____

The performance was in the (name of meet): _____

Location of meet: _____ Date of meet: _____, 20 _____

Sanctioned by: _____ State High School Association and (if interstate) by NFHS.

Full name of competitor for whom record is claimed (list all full names for a relay team):

_____ Age: ___ years ___ months
_____ Age: ___ years ___ months
_____ Age: ___ years ___ months
_____ Age: ___ years ___ months

This competitor(s) is an eligible member of _____ High School in _____
(city)

This high school is a member of the _____ State High School Association under whose rules the school competed.

The claimed record was: (time, height or distance): _____

Was this record established in competition limited exclusively to high school contestants?
Yes _____ No _____

> (**Note:** For a performance to be recognized as a national record, it shall be established in competition limited exclusively to high school contestants.)

Did this meet involve five or more high schools?
Yes _____ No _____

> (**Note:** For a performance to be recognized as a national record, it shall be established in a meet involving five or more schools.)

If a track event, was the time recorded by a fully automatic timing (FAT) system?
Yes _____ No _____

> (**Note:** For a performance to be recognized as a national record, the time shall be recorded by a fully automatic timing [FAT] system.)

Signature: _____   _____
(Competitor or captain for a relay team)   *(Principal of the high school)*

STATEMENT OF REFEREE. The competitive conditions were in compliance with NFHS rules. An anemometer, as prescribed by the rules, was used. There was no tailwind exceeding 4.473 miles per hour (or 2 meters per second) at any time during the record performance for races up to and including 200 meters, plus long and triple jumps. I officially endorse this application for a national record.

(**Note:** The referee should state any exceptions he or she desires to make to the foregoing statement. He or she should also describe the conditions of the track or field, the force and direction of the wind, slope of landing area and any other matters which might in any way influence the results of the performance.)

Anemometer reading (actual miles per hour): _____ ,or_____ meters per second

Weather: _____

Track and field condition: _____

Referee: _____ Street address: _____

City and state: _____

ENDORSEMENT BY STATE ASSOCIATION EXECUTIVE OFFICER

This interscholastic track and field meet was sanctioned by the home state high school association and conducted in compliance with NFHS rules.
Officer: _____, _____
State High School Association

ACTION OF THE NFHS NATIONAL RECORDS COMMITTEE

This application was considered by the NFHS National Records Committee on:
Date: _____, 20_____

The performance was accepted as a national record.   Yes _____ No_____

Chair, NFHS National Records Committee: _____

CERTIFICATION IN SUPPORT OF PERFORMANCE RECORD

CERTIFICATION BY SURVEYOR. I certify that the race course over which the event was conducted was measured in accordance with NFHS rules and found to be official. The course consisted of _____ laps, each measuring exactly _____ meters.

Surveyor: _____

CERTIFICATION BY FIELD REFEREE OR HEAD FIELD JUDGE. I certify that the implement used by the competitor, plus all other equipment and the competition area was in compliance with NFHS rules.

Field referee or head field judge: _____

CERTIFICATION BY FAT TIMING DEVICE OPERATOR AND CHIEF FINISH EVALUATOR. We certify that a fully automatic timing (FAT) system was operable and that the recorded time is correct and official.

Time: _____ Timing device operator: _____ Chief finish evaluator: _____

CERTIFICATION BY STARTER. I certify that the race had a fair start with no advantage provided to the competitor.

Starter: _____

CERTIFICATION BY REFEREE AND FIELD EVENT JUDGE. We certify that the measurement was recorded in accordance with NFHS rules.

Event: _____

Distance or height: _____

Referee: _____

Field event judge: _____

CERTIFICATION OF WITNESSES. We certify that we were present when the claimed record was made. All competitive conditions were in accordance with NFHS rules. We support the record application and recommend its acceptance.

Meet director: _____

Scorer: _____

Finish or field judge: _____

Finish or field judge: _____

AFFIDAVIT OF AUTHENTICITY. (By the meet director, scorer or other major meet official.)

STATE OF: _____
_____ SS
_____ County

I certify the signatures included on this application are authentic and valid.

Signature: _____

Official position: _____

Address: _____
      (Street)   *(City)*   *(State)*   *(Zip)*

> **SPORTSMANSHIP STATEMENT:** The NFHS National Records Committee is pleased to recognize outstanding achievements by teams and individuals. Although it is impossible to determine intent when marks are established, the committee strongly encourages recognition of performances in the true spirit of interscholastic competition. Running up scores or embarrassing an opponent for the primary purpose of inclusion in the *National High School Sports Record Book* is not consistent with the ideals of good sportsmanship.

From *Officiating Track & Field and Cross Country*, ASEP, 2005, Champaign, IL: Human Kinetics.

Cross Country Team Instruction Sheet

Meet: _____

Date: _____ Time: _____

Directions to meet location: _____
_____
_____
_____

Course information *(length, surface, terrain, markings, etc.):* _____
_____
_____
_____
_____

Course open for warm-ups at what time? _____
Note: Please arrive early enough to walk the course and ask questions before the meet.

Course map enclosed? *(circle one)*   *YES   NO*

Special ground rules *(due to unusual terrain, other circumstance, etc.):*
_____
_____

Explanation of finish: _____
_____
_____
_____
_____

Chute diagram *(include sketch here or attach copy to this form):*

Location and use of dressing rooms, locker assignments and showers *(if available):*

_____

_____

_____

Restricted areas: _____

_____

_____

_____

Uniform and spike requirements: _____

_____

_____

_____

Additional instructions for coaches/team managers: _____

_____

_____

_____

Instructions for spectators: _____

_____

_____

_____

Position of competitors' numbers and method of securing: _____

_____

_____

Is wireless communication allowed? *(circle one)*   YES   NO

Will water be available on the course? *(circle one)*   YES   NO

From *Officiating Track & Field and Cross Country,* ASEP, 2005, Champaign, IL: Human Kinetics.

Cross Country Officials' Instruction Sheet

Meet: _____

Date: _____ Time: _____

Referee

❑ Meet with meet manager to discuss instructions, terms and conditions related to the operation of the meet.

❑ Meet with head official and all head meet officials (scorers, finish judges, umpires, starter, clerks, etc.).

❑ Hold premeet meeting with all head coaches/captains (30 minutes prior to the start of the race) to discuss uniforms, jewelry, finish procedures, good sportsmanship, etc. If the referee is unable to hold this meeting, the assistant referee or the head official will conduct the meeting in place of the referee.

❑ At the conclusion of the race, follow state association meet scoring procedures. When final race results are certified, signed and timed by the referee, the meet manager will receive a copy of the results to be posted.

❑ Remain at the park meet site for 30 minutes after the race to address and review any appeals. If an appeal is filed, provide the coach with a form to address the appeal in writing. The appeal will then be reviewed immediately by the games committee at the meet site. No appeals will be discussed after the 30-minute timeframe.

❑ Submit report to the state association cross country administrator and the lead official following the meet. The report should include information related to the operation of the meet and a review of the officials' performance.

Assistant Referee

❑ Assist the referee in any manner that will aid in the running of the meet, as necessary.

❑ Meet with umpires prior to the meet and oversee umpires and their placement on the course.

❑ Conduct premeet meeting if the referee is not able to do so.

Umpires

❑ Meet with assistant referee prior to meet to receive positions on the course and meet instructions.

❑ During the meet observe runners to ensure they are running the proper course; to check for interference which may occur between competitors, noncompetitors, fans, etc. and to check for unsportsmanlike or unacceptable conduct. Report any infractions observed during the meet to the assistant referee immediately following each race.

Starter

❑ Meet with meet manager, referee and the head official to discuss meet responsibilities.

❑ Observe all activities at the starting line and the clerks of the course.

❑ When the meet announcer has finished instructions and has turned the race over, assume position on the ladder, verify that you are visible to the timers and other necessary personnel, verify that clerk/assistant starters are in position and begin race.

❑ Remain on ladder until all runners have run beyond the 100-meter area in the event that a recall may be in order.

❑ Serve in any other capacity as designated by the referee prior to the meet.

Clerk or Assistant Starters

❑ Meet with referee, starter and head official approximately one hour prior to the start of the first race to discuss meet duties.

❑ Walk starting line thirty minutes prior to start of meet to become familiar with assigned starting boxes.

❑ Meet with meet announcer to review meet time schedule.

❑ Clear starting boxes 20 minutes prior to start of race and begin checking in the teams and individual runners.

❑ Clear all coaches and nonparticipants from the starting boxes two minutes prior to race and signal to starter that the boxes have been cleared.

❑ Position as necessary for start of race.

❑ Serve in any other capacity as designated by the referee prior to the meet.

From *Officiating Track & Field and Cross Country*, ASEP, 2005, Champaign, IL: Human Kinetics.

Violation Report

Directions: This report shall be completed and signed by the observing umpire when the infractions occur in running events. Do not use for false starts. All completed reports from sectional, district, regional and state meets must be forwarded to the state high school association at the conclusion of the meet.

Meet: *(circle one)*   *SECTIONAL   DISTRICT   REGIONAL   STATE*

BOYS   GIRLS

Location: *(city)* _____ **Date:** _____

Event: _____ **Heat:** _____ **Class:** _____

Name of participant: _____ **Number:** _____

School: _____ **Jersey color:** _____ **Lane:** _____

Infraction: *(Check infraction on "Summary of Running Rules Infractions Reporting Form" and circle the number below)*

1 2 3 4 5 6 7 8 9 10 11 12 13

14 15 16 17 18 19 20 21 22 23 24

25 26 27 28 29 30 31 32 33 34

35 36 37 38 39 40 41 42 43 44

For relays:

Which exchange? _____

If number 23, was foul before or after the zone? _____

Signature of reporting official: _____

For referee use only:

Referee's decision: *(check one)*   ____ *DISQUALIFIED FROM EVENT*

____ *DISQUALIFIED FROM MEET*

____ NOT DISQUALIFIED

____ *OTHER:* _____

Signature of referee: _____ **Date**: _____

From *Officiating Track & Field and Cross Country*, ASEP, 2005, Champaign, IL: Human Kinetics.

Summary of Running Rules Infractions Reporting Form

Event: _____ Date: _____

Name of participant: _____ Number: _____

School: _____

Infraction

1. ____ Steps on or over inside lane line on a curve for three or more consecutive steps
2. ____ Interference by a competitor
3. ____ Interference by a noncompetitor
4. ____ Improving competitor's position by running on or inside track curb or outside assigned lane
5. ____ Finish in the wrong lane in races requiring assigned lanes

Hurdler

6. ____ Did not attempt to clear each hurdle
7. ____ Deliberately knocks down a hurdle by hand or foot
8. ____ Advances or trails a leg or foot alongside or below the height of the hurdle gate
9. ____ Runs over a hurdle not in the assigned lane
10. ____ Runs around a hurdle
11. ____ Impedes another hurdler

Unfair Act

12. ____ Interference with another competitor
13. ____ Competitor coached or assisted by an individual in a restricted area
14. ____ Competitors join hands or grasp each other any time during a race
15. ____ Competitor is paced or assisted by a teammate
16. ____ Competitor uses any aid during the race
17. ____ Competitor views video or uses wireless device prior to completion

Relay Teams

18. ____ Violation of substitution rule
19. ____ Failure to carry a baton
20. ____ Failure to position within an acceleration zone
21. ____ Failure to position within the exchange zone
22. ____ Failure to pass baton in the exchange zone
23. ____ Baton not handed between runners
24. ____ Incoming runner pushes outgoing runner
25. ____ Throwing the baton after race has ended
26. ____ Wearing gloves during competition

Uniforms

27. ____ Failure to wear the school uniform (including assigned contestant number)
28. ____ Alters contestant number
29. ____ Failure of relay team to wear same color and design school uniform
30. ____ Illegal visible apparel (including jewelry)
31. ____ Violation of manufacturer's logo or trademark restrictions
32. ____ Failure to wear shoes
33. ____ Removal of uniform (warning for first offense)

Unsportsmanlike Conduct

34. ____ Conduct that is unethical or dishonorable
35. ____ Taunting or criticizing an opponent
36. ____ Disrespectfully addressing an official
37. ____ While participating as a contestant, using profanity directed toward another person
38. ____ Any flagrant behavior or intentional contact
39. ____ Using tobacco
40. ____ Removal of uniform (second offense)

Unacceptable Conduct

41. ____ Willful failure to follow directions of a meet official
42. ____ Use of profanity that is not directed at anyone
43. ____ Any action that discredits an individual or his or her school

Other

44. ____ Description: _____

From *Officiating Track & Field and Cross Country,* ASEP, 2005, Champaign, IL: Human Kinetics.

Field Event Checklist

Directions: Use the following form to inspect each field event area and ensure the legality of the area and the safety of the competitors.

Meet: _____

Date: _____ Time: _____

Pole vault	Comments
Landing pad (19' 8" wide, 20' 2" deep; back of box 16' 5"; runway 130')	
Planting box	
Standards and crossbar (13' 8" – 14' 10")	
Surrounding area	
Weigh-in of athletes	
Coaching box	
High jump	**Comments**
Landing pit (16' by 8')	
Standards and crossbar (12' apart; bar can vary in length)	
Surrounding area	

Long jump and triple jump	Comments
Landing pit (9' by 15')	
Runway (130')	
Take-off marks (8' and 28' and 32')	
Rakes, shovels	
Brooms	
Sand level	
Surrounding area	

Shot put	Comments
Circle sector and markings	
Surrounding area	
Weight implements	

Discus throw	Comments
Cage	
Circle sector and markings	
Surrounding area	
Weight implements	

From *Officiating Track & Field and Cross Country,* ASEP, 2005, Champaign, IL: Human Kinetics.

Pole-Vault Event

Meet: _____   Date: _____   Time: _____

Qualifying standard: _____ **Starting height: :** _____ **Meet record:** _____

0 = Successful trial   P = Passed trial   X = Failure of trial

Competitors				Pole vault			Height of bar						
No.	Name	Grade	School	Vaulter's weight	Pole rating	Coach's initials							

Place	Pts	Distance/ height	No.	Name	Grade	School	Official's initials

From *Officiating Track & Field and Cross Country*, ASEP, 2005, Champaign, IL: Human Kinetics.

Pole-Vault Facility Checklist

Meet: _____

Date: _____ Time: _____

Pole-Vault Landing Area

❏ *Width*: 19 feet, 8 inches minimum beyond the back of standard bases

❏ *Length*: 16 feet, 5 inches minimum from back of the box to the back of the pit

❏ Uniform top pad must cover all sections

❏ Maximum of 3 inches only is allowed between back of box and the pit

❏ Minimum of 2 inches of padding must cover hard and unyielding surfaces around the pit including between the box and the pit

❏ Front edge of the box cannot extend above the grade of the runway surface

❏ All parts of standard bases must be covered by protector pads

❏ Width between the crossbar pins should not be less than 13 feet, 8 inches or exceed 14 feet, 8 inches

Vaulting Poles

❏ Competitor's weight must be at or below the manufacturer's pole rating. Manufacturers must include the pole rating in numbers at least 3/4 inch tall in a contrasting color located within or above the top handhold position. Manufacturers must also provide a 1-inch circular band indicating the maximum top hand-hold position.

❏ Vaulter's weight cannot exceed the weight rating of the pole. The vaulter's weight should be at or less than the test weight of the pole.

From *Officiating Track & Field and Cross Country*, ASEP, 2005, Champaign, IL: Human Kinetics.

Cross Country Meet Director Checklist

Meet: _____

Date: _____ Time: _____

Premeet

- ❏ Check site plans and permit, sanctions, date, time, facility provisions, budget
- ❏ Check schools and coaches
- ❏ Order contestant numbers and pins
- ❏ Hire officials and workers; plan for medical help
- ❏ Send information to schools
- ❏ Arrange advance publicity
- ❏ Check trophies and medals for accuracy
- ❏ Check insurance policies for updated coverage
- ❏ Secure restroom facilities
- ❏ Prepare the course and finish chute; prepare signs, flags and course markers; identify restricted areas on the course
- ❏ Set time schedule for coaches' meeting, officials' meeting, anthem, team introductions and races

Meet Day

- ❏ Team entries and envelopes, headquarter signs, meet permit, insurance forms, cellular phone
- ❏ Appeals forms, officials' and workers' sign-in sheets, job descriptions, vests, snacks
- ❏ Extra course maps for teams and large map for display; timing charts
- ❏ Finish tickets and team scoring envelopes
- ❏ Contestant number and order-of-finish chart
- ❏ Tape recorder (extra batteries and tape)
- ❏ PA system, megaphones, U.S. flag, national anthem and music on tape or CD
- ❏ Seiko timer or printer (extra watches, tapes), camcorder, ladder
- ❏ Pistol, shells, umpire flags, rules book, infraction cards
- ❏ Bulletin board, charts, marking pens, tacks, tape, rubber binders, table and chairs
- ❏ Scissors, stapler, paper clips, extra contestant numbers and pins, small hand tools
- ❏ Awards and certificates, finish chute, covers for leading stakes
- ❏ Course signs, markers, hammer, measuring wheel, painting mechanism, paint
- ❏ Starting line, alley stakes, markings, ball of string, heavy hammer, shovel and rake
- ❏ Flags, pennants, cones, stakes, crowd control provisions, gas blower, generator and fuel
- ❏ Refuse bags, Kleenex, toilet paper, flashlight, provisions for inclement weather

Postmeet

- ❏ Report results to area media and place information and results on the appropriate Web sites
- ❏ Mail meet summaries to each participating school

From *Officiating Track & Field and Cross Country*, ASEP, 2005, Champaign, IL: Human Kinetics.

APPENDIX B

Decathlon and Heptathlon Scoring Tables

The following tables are NFHS-approved scoring tables for use in boys' decathlons and girls' heptathlons. For further information, please contact your state association.

Boys' Decathlon

The boys' decathlon shall consist of 10 events held on two consecutive days in the following order, unless state association rules apply:

First Day

1. 100-meter dash
2. Long jump
3. Shot put
4. High jump
5. 400-meter dash

Second Day

1. Triple jump or javelin
2. Discus
3. 110-meter high hurdles
4. Pole vault
5. 1,600-meter run

100-Meter Dash

Points	Seconds	Points	Seconds	Points	Seconds
932	10.5	520	12.3	213	14.1
905	10.6	501	12.4	198	14.2
879	10.7	482	12.5	184	14.3
853	10.8	463	12.6	170	14.4
823	10.9	444	12.7	156	14.5
804	11.0	426	12.8	142	14.6
780	11.1	408	12.9	128	14.7
756	11.2	390	13.0	114	14.8
733	11.3	373	13.1	101	14.9
710	11.4	356	13.2	88	15.0
687	11.5	339	13.3	75	15.1
665	11.6	322	13.4	49	15.3
643	11.7	306	13.5	36	15.4
622	11.8	290	13.6	24	15.5
601	11.9	274	13.7	12	15.6
580	12.0	258	13.8	0	15.7
560	12.1	243	13.9		
540	12.2	228	14.0		

Long Jump

Points	Meters	Feet/inches	Points	Meters	Feet/inches	Points	Meters	Feet/inches
921	7.50	24' 7-¼"	728	6.56	21' 6-¼"	505	5.56	18' 3"
917	7.48	24' 6-½"	723	6.54	12' 5-½"	503	5.55	18' 2-¾"
913	7.46	24' 5-¾"	719	6.52	21' ¾"	498	5.53	18' 2"
909	7.44	24' 5"	715	6.50	21' 4"	493	5.51	18' 1"
905	7.42	24' 4-¼"	710	6.48	21' 3-¼"	489	5.49	18' ¼"
901	7.40	24' 3-¼"	706	6.46	21' 2-¼"	484	5.47	17' 11-½"
897	7.38	24' 2-½"	701	6.44	2' 1-½"	479	5.45	17' 10-¾"

(continued)

Long Jump (continued)

Points	Meters	Feet/inches	Points	Meters	Feet/inches	Points	Meters	Feet/inches
895	7.37	24' 2"	697	6.42	21' ¾"	475	5.43	17' 10"
891	7.35	24' 1-½"	693	6.40	21' 0"	470	5.41	17' 9-¼"
998	7.33	24' ½"	688	6.38	20' 11-¼"	465	5.39	17' 8-½"
883	7.31	23' 11-¾"	684	6.36	20' 10-½"	460	5.37	17' 7-½"
881	7.30	23' 11-½"	680	6.34	20' 9-¾"	456	5.35	17' 6-¾"
877	7.28	23' 10-¾"	675	6.32	20' 8-¾"	451	5.33	17' 6"
875	7.27	23' 10-¼"	671	6.30	20' 8"	446	5.31	17' 5-¼"
871	7.25	23' 9-½"	666	6.28	20' 7-¼"	441	5.29	17' 4-½"
869	7.24	23' 9"	662	6.26	20' 6-½"	437	5.27	17' 3-¾"
865	7.22	23' 8-¼"	657	6.24	20' 5-¾"	432	5.25	17' 2-¾"
861	7.20	23' 7-½"	653	6.22	20' 5"	427	5.23	17' 2"
857	7.18	23' 6-¾"	648	6.20	20' 4"	423	5.21	17' 1-¾"
853	7.16	23' 6"	644	6.18	20' 3-¼"	418	5.19	17' 0"
848	7.14	23' 5-¼"	640	6.16	20' 2-½"	413	5.17	16' 11-¾"
844	7.12	23' 4-¼"	635	6.14	20' 1-¾"	408	5.15	16' 11"
840	7.10	23' 3-½"	631	6.12	20' 1"	403	5.12	16' 9-¾"
836	7.08	23' 2-¾"	626	6.10	20' ¼"	395	5.10	16' 9"
617	6.06	19' 10-½"	622	6.08	19' 11-½"	390	5.08	16' 8-¼"
832	7.06	23' 2"	617	6.06	19' 10-½"	385	5.06	16' 7-½"
828	7.04	23' 1-¼"	613	6.04	19' 9-¾"	381	5.04	16' 6-½"
824	7.02	23' ½"	608	6.02	19' 9"	376	5.02	16' 5-¾"
820	7.00	22' 11-½"	604	6.00	19' 8-¼"	371	5.00	16' 5"
816	6.98	22' 10-¾"	600	5.98	19' 7-½"	366	4.98	16' 4"
812	6.96	22' 10"	595	5.96	19' 6-¾"	361	4.96	16' 3"
808	6.94	22' 9-¼"	591	5.94	19' 6"	356	4.94	16' 2-½"
804	6.92	22' 8-½"	586	5.92	19' 5"	351	4.92	16' 1-¾"
800	6.90	22' 7-¾"	582	5.90	19' 4-¼"	346	4.90	16' 1"
796	6.88	22' 7"	577	5.88	19' 3-½"	341	4.88	16' 0"
791	6.86	22' 6"	573	5.86	19' 2-¾"	336	4.86	15' 11-½"
787	6.84	22' 5-¼"	568	5.84	19' 2"	331	4.84	15' 10-½"
782	6.82	22' 4-½"	564	5.82	19' 1-¼"	326	4.82	15' 9-¾"
778	6.80	22' 3-¾"	560	5.80	19' ¼"	321	4.80	15' 9"
774	6.78	22' 3"	555	5.78	18' 11-¾"	316	4.78	15' 8"
770	6.76	22' 2-¼"	551	5.76	18' 11"	311	4.76	15' 7-½"
765	6.74	22' 1-½"	546	5.74	18' 10-¼"	306	4.74	15' 6-¾"
761	6.72	22' ½"	542	5.72	18' 9-¼"	301	4.72	15' 5-¾"
757	6.70	21' 11-¾"	537	5.70	18' 8-½"	296	4.70	15' 5"
753	6.68	21' 11"	533	5.68	18' 7-¾"	291	4.68	15' 4-¼"
748	6.66	21' 10-¼"	528	5.66	18' 7"	286	4.66	15' 3-½"
744	6.64	21' 9-½"	523	5.64	18' 6-¼"	281	4.64	15' 2-¾"
740	6.62	21' 8-¾"	519	5.62	18' 5-½"	276	4.62	15' 2"
736	6.60	21' 7-¾"	514	5.60	18' 4-¾"	271	4.60	15' 1-¼"
732	6.58	21' 7"	510	5.58	18' 3-¾"	266	4.58	15' ¼"

Shot Put

Points	Meters	Feet/inches	Points	Meters	Feet/inches	Points	Meters	Feet/inches
970	18.19	59' 8-1/4"	731	14.04	46' 3/4"	491	10.42	34' 2-1/4"
962	18.04	59' 2-1/4"	723	13.92	45' 8"	483	10.30	33' 9-1/2"
954	17.89	58' 8-1/4"	715	13.79	45' 3"	475	10.20	33' 5-1/2"
946	17.75	58' 2-3/4"	707	13.67	44' 10-3/4"	467	10.09	33' 2-1/4"
938	17.60	57' 9"	699	13.54	44' 5"	459	10.01	32' 9-1/2"
930	17.46	57' 3-1/2"	691	13.41	44' 0"	451	9.88	32' 5-3/4"
922	17.32	56' 9-3/4"	683	13.28	43' 6-3/4"	443	9.77	32' 1-1/2"
914	17.17	56' 4"	675	13.16	43' 2-1/4"	435	9.66	31' 10-1/4"
906	17.03	55' 10-1/2"	667	13.06	42' 9"	427	9.56	31' 8-1/4"
898	16.89	55' 5"	659	12.91	42' 4-1/4"	419	9.45	31' 0"
890	16.75	54' 11-1/2"	651	12.79	41' 11-1/2"	411	9.34	30' 8-3/4"
883	16.62	54' 6-1/4"	643	12.66	41' 6-1/2"	403	9.23	30' 4-1/4"
875	16.48	54' 3/4"	635	12.54	41' 1-3/4"	395	9.12	29' 0"
867	16.34	53' 7-1/4"	627	12.42	40' 9"	387	9.02	29' 7"
859	16.20	53' 1-3/4"	619	12.30	40' 4-1/4"	379	8.92	29' 3-1/4"
851	16.06	52' 8-1/4"	611	12.18	39' 11-1/2"	371	8.82	28' 11-1/4"
843	15.92	52' 2-3/4"	603	12.06	39' 6-3/4"	363	8.72	28' 7-1/4"
835	15.78	51' 9-1/4"	595	11.94	39' 2"	355	8.62	28' 3-1/2"
827	15.65	51' 4-1/4"	587	11.82	38' 9-1/2"	347	8.52	27' 11-1/2"
819	15.51	50' 10-3/4"	579	11.70	38' 4-3/4"	339	8.42	27' 7-1/2"
811	15.37	50' 5-1/4"	571	11.58	38' 0"	331	8.32	27' 3-1/2"
803	15.24	50' 0"	563	11.46	37' 7-1/4"	323	8.22	26' 11-3/4"
795	15.10	49' 6-1/2"	555	11.34	37' 2-1/2"	315	8.12	26' 7-3/4"
787	14.97	49' 1-1/2"	547	11.22	36' 9-3/4"	307	8.02	26' 3-3/4"
779	14.84	48' 8-1/4"	539	11.10	36' 5"	299	7.92	25' 11-3/4"
771	14.70	48' 2-3/4"	531	10.98	36' 1/4"	291	7.82	25' 7-3/4"
763	14.57	47' 9-3/4"	523	10.87	35' 8"	283	7.72	25' 3-3/4"
755	14.44	47' 4-1/2"	515	10.76	35' 3-3/4"	275	7.63	25' 0"
747	14.31	46' 11-1/2"	507	10.64	34' 11"			
739	14.17	46' 6"	499	10.53	34' 6-1/2"			

High Jump

Points	Meters	Feet/inches	Points	Meters	Feet/inches	Points	Meters	Feet/inches
1000	2.17	7' 1-1/2"	662	1.78	5' 10"	303	1.41	4' 7-3/4"
992	2.16	7' 1"	643	1.76	5' 9-1/4"	293	1.40	4' 7-1/4"
975	2.14	7' 1/4"	625	1.74	5' 8-1/2"	283	1.39	4' 7"
959	2.12	6' 11-1/2"	607	1.72	5' 7-3/4"	273	1.38	4' 6-1/2"
942	2.10	6' 10-3/4"	588	1.70	5' 7"	263	1.37	4' 6"
925	2.08	6' 10"	569	1.68	5' 6-1/4"	252	1.36	4' 5-3/4"
909	2.06	6' 9-1/4"	550	1.66	5' 5-1/2"	242	1.35	4' 5-1/4"
891	2.04	6' 8-1/4"	531	1.64	5' 4-3/4"	231	1.34	4' 5"
874	2.02	6' 7-1/2"	512	1.62	5' 4"	220	1.33	4' 4-1/2"
857	2.00	6' 6-3/4"	493	1.60	5' 3-1/4"	210	1.32	4' 4"
840	1.98	6' 6"	473	1.58	5' 2-1/4"	199	1.31	4' 3-3/4"
822	1.96	6' 5-1/4"	453	1.56	5' 1-1/2"	189	1.30	4' 3-1/4"

(continued)

High Jump (continued)

Points	Meters	Feet/inches	Points	Meters	Feet/inches	Points	Meters	Feet/inches
804	1.94	6' 4-½"	434	1.54	5' ¾"	178	1.29	4' 3"
788	1.92	6' 3-½"	414	1.52	5' 0"	167	1.28	4' 2-½"
769	1.90	6' 2-¾"	394	1.50	4' 11-¾"	156	1.27	4' 2-¼"
751	1.88	6' 2"	374	1.48	4' 10-½"	146	1.26	4' 1-¾"
734	1.86	6' 1-¼"	354	1.46	4' 9-¾"	135	1.25	4' 1-¼"
716	1.84	6' ½"	344	1.44	4' 8-¾"	124	1.24	4' 1"
698	1.82	5' 11-¾"	324	1.43	4' 8-½"	113	1.23	4' ½"
680	1.80	5' 11"	314	1.42	4' 8"	101	1.22	4' ¼"

400-Meter Dash

Seconds	Points	Seconds	Points	Seconds	Points
48.0	893	56.0	566	64.0	316
48.2	889	56.2	559	64.2	311
48.4	880	56.4	552	64.4	306
48.6	871	56.6	544	64.6	300
48.8	861	56.8	537	64.8	294
49.0	852	57.0	531	65.0	289
49.2	842	57.2	524	65.2	284
49.4	833	57.4	517	65.4	278
49.6	824	57.6	511	65.6	273
49.8	814	57.8	504	65.8	268
50.0	805	58.0	497	66.0	263
50.2	797	58.2	491	66.2	258
50.4	788	58.4	484	66.4	253
50.6	779	58.6	477	66.6	248
50.8	770	58.8	470	66.8	243
51.0	762	59.0	464	67.0	238
51.2	753	59.2	458	67.2	233
51.4	744	59.4	451	67.4	228
51.6	736	59.6	445	67.6	223
51.8	728	59.8	439	67.8	218
52.0	720	60.0	433	68.0	213
52.2	712	60.2	426	68.2	208
52.4	703	60.4	420	68.4	203
52.6	695	60.6	414	68.6	198
52.8	687	60.8	408	68.8	194
53.0	679	61.0	402	69.0	189
53.2	671	61.2	396	69.2	184
53.4	663	61.4	390	69.4	180
53.6	655	61.6	384	69.6	175
53.8	648	61.8	378	69.8	170
54.0	640	62.0	372	70.0	166
54.2	633	62.2	366	70.2	161
54.4	625	62.4	360	70.4	157
54.6	617	62.6	354	70.6	152

(continued)

Seconds	Points	Seconds	Points	Seconds	Points
54.8	610	62.8	349	70.8	148
55.0	603	63.0	343	71.0	143
55.2	596	63.2	337	71.2	139
55.4	588	63.4	332	71.4	135
55.6	580	63.6	326	71.6	130
55.8	573	63.8	321	71.8	126

Triple Jump

Points	Meters	Feet/inches	Points	Meters	Feet/inches	Points	Meters	Feet/inches
1200	18.43	60' 5-¾"	830	14.50	47' 7"	460	11.04	36' 2-½"
1190	18.31	60' 0"	820	14.40	47' 3"	450	10.95	35' 11-¾"
1180	18.20	59' 8-¾"	810	14.30	46' 11"	440	10.87	35' 8"
1170	18.09	59' 4-¼"	800	14.20	46' 7-¼"	430	10.78	35' 4-½"
1160	17.98	58' 11-¾"	790	14.10	46' 3-¼"	420	10.69	35' 1"
1150	17.87	58' 7-½"	780	14.00	45' 11-¼"	410	10.61	34' 9-¾"
1140	17.76	58' 3-¼"	770	13.91	45' 7-½"	400	10.52	34' 6-¼"
1130	17.65	57' 10-¾"	760	13.81	45' 3-¾"	390	10.44	34' 3"
1120	17.54	57' 6-½"	750	13.71	44' 11-¾"	380	10.35	33' 11-½"
1110	17.43	57' 2-¼"	740	13.61	44' 7-¾"	370	10.27	33' 8-½"
1100	17.32	56' 9-¾"	730	13.52	44' 4-¼"	360	10.19	33' 5-¼"
1090	17.21	56' 5-½"	720	13.42	44' ¼"	350	10.10	33' 1-¾"
1080	17.10	56' 1-¼"	710	13.32	43' 8-¼"	340	10.02	32' 10"
1070	16.99	55' 9"	700	13.25	43' 5-½"	330	9.94	32' 7-¼"
1060	16.89	55' 5"	690	13.13	43' 1"	320	9.85	32' 3-¾"
1050	16.78	55' ¾"	680	13.04	42' 9-¼"	310	9.77	32' ½"
1040	16.67	54' 8-½"	670	12.94	42' 5-½"	300	9.69	31' 9-½"
1030	16.56	54' 4"	660	12.85	42' 2"	290	9.61	31' 6-¼"
1020	16.46	54' ¼"	650	12.76	41' 10-½"	280	9.53	31' 3-¼"
1010	16.35	53' 7-¾"	640	12.66	41' 6-½"	270	9.45	31' 0"
1000	16.25	53' 3-¾"	630	12.57	41' 3"	260	9.37	30' 8-¾"
990	16.14	52' 11-½"	620	12.48	40' 11-½"	250	9.29	30' 5-¾"
980	16.03	52' 7-¼"	610	12.38	40' 7-½"	240	9.21	30' 2-½"
970	15.93	52' 3"	600	12.29	40' 4"	230	9.13	29' 11-½"
960	15.82	51' 10-½"	590	12.20	40' ½"	220	9.05	29' 8-¼"
950	15.72	51' 6-½"	580	12.11	39' 8-¾"	210	8.97	29' 5-¼"
940	15.62	51' 2-¾"	570	12.02	39' 5"	200	8.89	29' 2"
930	15.51	50' 10-¼"	560	11.93	39' 1-¾"	190	8.81	28' 11"
920	15.41	50' 6-½"	550	11.84	38' 10"	179	8.73	28' 7-¼"
910	15.31	50' 2-½"	540	11.75	38' 6-½"	170	8.66	28' 5"
900	15.21	49' 11"	530	11.66	38' 3"	160	8.58	28' 1-¾"
890	15.10	49' 6-¼"	520	11.57	37' 11-½"	149	8.50	27' 10-¾"
880	15.00	49' 2-¼"	510	11.48	37' 8"	139	8.42	27' 7-¼"
870	14.90	48' 10-¾"	500	11.39	37' 4-½"	128	8.34	27' 4-½"
860	14.80	48' 6-¾"	490	11.30	37' ¾"	120	8.28	27' 2"
850	14.70	48' 2-¾"	480	11.21	36' 9-½"	108	8.19	26' 10-½"
840	14.60	47' 11"	470	11.13	36' 6-¼"	100	8.13	26' 8-¼"

Discus

Points	Meters	Feet	Points	Meters	Feet	Points	Meters	Feet
943	53.63	176'	714	41.44	136'	458	29.29	96'
937	53.33	175'	708	41.14	135'	451	28.98	95'
931	52.99	174'	702	40.82	134'	444	28.66	94'
925	52.73	173'	696	40.52	133'	436	28.34	93'
918	52.43	172'	690	40.22	132'	429	28.04	92'
911	52.15	171'	684	39.90	131'	422	27.74	91'
904	51.82	170'	678	39.60	130'	415	27.58	90'
899	51.52	169'	672	39.30	129'	407	27.41	89'
893	51.18	168'	666	39.00	128'	400	26.83	88'
888	50.90	167'	659	38.66	127'	393	26.54	87'
883	50.62	166'	653	38.36	126'	386	26.25	86'
877	50.28	165'	647	38.06	125'	378	25.92	85'
872	49.98	164'	641	37.76	124'	370	25.60	84'
867	49.70	163'	635	37.48	123'	362	25.27	83'
861	49.38	162'	629	37.18	122'	355	24.99	82'
855	49.04	161'	623	36.84	121'	347	24.67	81'
850	48.76	160'	617	36.60	120'	339	24.35	80'
845	48.48	159'	611	36.30	119'	332	24.08	79'
839	48.14	158'	604	35.96	118'	324	23.77	78'
834	47.86	157'	598	35.68	117'	316	23.45	77'
828	47.52	156'	592	35.40	116'	308	23.15	76'
823	47.24	155'	585	35.06	115'	300	22.84	75'
817	46.92	154'	579	34.76	114'	292	22.54	74'
812	46.64	153'	572	34.44	113'	284	22.23	73'
806	46.32	152'	566	34.16	112'	276	21.93	72'
801	46.04	151'	559	33.84	111'	268	21.63	71'
795	45.72	150'	552	33.52	110'	260	21.33	70'
789	45.40	149'	546	33.24	109'	252	21.03	69'
783	45.08	148'	539	32.92	108'	244	20.75	68'
778	44.88	147'	533	32.64	107'	236	20.45	67'
772	44.48	146'	526	32.32	106'	227	20.13	66'
767	44.22	145'	519	32.00	105'	219	19.84	65'
761	43.90	144'	513	31.74	104'	210	19.52	64'
755	43.58	143'	506	31.42	103'	201	19.21	63'
749	43.26	142'	499	31.10	102'	193	18.92	62'
743	42.96	141'	492	30.78	101'	184	18.61	61'
738	42.70	140'	485	30.48	100'	175	18.30	60'
732	42.38	139'	478	30.16	99'	166	17.99	59'
726	42.06	138'	472	29.89	98'	157	17.69	58'
720	41.76	137'	464	29.54	97'	148	17.39	57'

110-Meter Hurdles

Seconds	Points	Seconds	Points	Seconds	Points
13.1	1080	18.2	568	23.3	279
13.2	1066	18.3	561	23.4	275
13.3	1052	18.4	554	23.5	271
13.4	1039	18.5	547	23.6	266
13.5	1036	18.6	540	23.7	262
13.6	1013	18.7	533	23.8	258
13.7	1000	18.8	526	23.9	253
13.8	987	18.9	519	24.0	249
13.9	974	19.0	512	24.1	245
14.0	962	19.1	506	24.2	241
14.1	950	19.2	499	24.3	237
14.2	938	19.3	493	24.4	233
14.3	926	19.4	487	24.5	229
14.4	914	19.5	480	24.6	225
14.5	903	19.6	474	24.7	221
14.6	892	19.7	468	24.8	217
14.7	881	19.8	461	24.9	213
14.8	870	19.9	455	25.0	209
14.9	859	20.0	449	25.1	205
15.0	848	20.1	443	25.2	202
15.1	837	20.2	438	25.3	198
15.2	827	20.3	432	25.4	194
15.3	817	20.4	426	25.5	191
15.4	807	20.5	420	25.6	187
15.5	797	20.6	415	25.7	183
15.6	787	20.7	409	25.8	180
15.7	777	20.8	403	25.9	176
15.8	767	20.9	398	26.0	173
15.9	757	21.0	394	26.1	169
16.0	748	21.1	387	26.2	166
16.1	739	21.2	381	26.3	162
16.2	730	21.3	376	26.4	159
16.3	721	21.4	371	26.5	156
16.4	712	21.5	366	26.6	152
16.5	703	21.6	361	26.7	149
16.6	694	21.7	356	26.8	145
16.7	685	21.8	350	26.9	142
16.8	676	21.9	345	27.0	138
16.9	668	22.0	340	27.1	135
17.0	660	22.1	335	27.2	132
17.1	652	22.2	331	27.3	129
17.2	645	22.3	326	27.4	126
17.3	637	22.4	321	27.5	123
17.4	629	22.5	316	27.6	119

(continued)

110-Meter Hurdles (continued)

Seconds	Points	Seconds	Points	Seconds	Points
17.5	621	22.6	312	27.7	116
17.6	613	22.7	307	27.8	113
17.7	605	22.8	302	27.9	110
17.8	597	22.9	297	28.0	107
17.9	590	23.0	293	28.1	104
18.0	582	23.1	288	28.2	101
18.1	575	23.2	284		

Pole Vault

Points	Meters	Feet/inches	Points	Meters	Feet/inches	Points	Meters	Feet/inches
1000	4.78	15' 8"	804	3.99	13' 1"	587	3.20	10' 6"
993	4.75	15' 7"	796	3.96	13' 0"	581	3.18	10' 5"
989	4.73	15' 6"	791	3.94	12' 11"	572	3.15	10' 4"
981	4.70	15' 5"	783	3.91	12' 10"	567	3.13	10' 3"
974	4.67	15' 4"	777	3.89	12' 9"	558	3.10	10' 2"
969	4.65	15' 3"	769	3.86	12' 8"	549	3.07	10' 1"
962	4.62	15' 2"	764	3.84	12' 7"	543	3.05	10' 0"
957	4.60	15' 1"	757	3.81	12' 6"	534	3.02	9' 11"
950	4.57	15' 0"	752	3.79	12' 5"	528	3.00	9' 10"
945	4.55	14' 11"	744	3.76	12' 4"	519	2.97	9' 9"
937	4.52	14' 10"	736	3.73	12' 3"	513	2.95	9' 8"
932	4.50	14' 9"	730	3.71	12' 2"	504	2.92	9' 7"
925	4.47	14' 8"	722	3.68	12' 1"	498	2.90	9' 6"
920	4.45	14' 7"	717	3.66	12' 0"	489	2.87	9' 5"
913	4.42	14' 6"	708	3.63	11' 11"	479	2.84	9' 4"
909	4.40	14' 5"	703	3.61	11' 10"	473	2.82	9' 3"
901	4.37	14' 4"	694	3.58	11' 9"	464	2.79	9' 2"
894	4.34	14' 3"	689	3.56	11' 8"	458	2.77	9' 1"
889	4.32	14' 2"	681	3.53	11' 7"	448	2.74	9' 0"
881	4.29	14' 1"	675	3.51	11' 6"	442	2.72	8' 11"
876	4.27	14' 0"	667	3.48	11' 5"	432	2.69	8' 10"
869	4.24	13' 11"	661	3.46	11' 4"	426	2.67	8' 9"
864	4.22	13' 10"	652	3.43	11' 3"	416	2.64	8' 8"
856	4.19	13' 9"	644	3.40	11' 2"	406	2.61	8' 7"
851	4.17	13' 8"	638	3.38	11' 1"	400	2.59	8' 6"
842	4.14	13' 7"	630	3.35	11' 0"	390	2.56	8' 5"
837	4.12	13' 6"	624	3.33	10' 11"	384	2.54	8' 4"
830	4.09	13' 5"	615	3.30	10' 10"	374	2.51	8' 2"
825	4.07	13' 4"	610	3.28	10' 9"	358	2.46	8' 1"
817	4.04	13' 3"	601	3.25	10' 8"	351	2.44	8' 0"
809	4.01	13' 2"	595	3.23	10' 7"			

1,600-Meter Run

Minutes	Points	Minutes	Points	Minutes	Points
3:51	1097	4:46	617	5:41	301
3:52	1086	4:47	610	5:42	297
3:53	1075	4:48	603	5:43	292
3:54	1064	4:49	596	5:44	287
3:55	1053	4:50	589	5:45	282
3:56	1043	4:51	583	5:46	277
3:57	1032	4:52	576	5:47	273
3:58	1022	4:53	569	5:48	268
3:59	1012	4:54	563	5:49	264
4:00	1002	4:55	556	5:50	259
4:01	992	4:56	550	5:51	255
4:02	982	4:57	543	5:52	250
4:03	972	4:58	537	5:53	246
4:04	962	4:59	531	5:54	242
4:05	952	5:00	525	5:55	237
4:06	943	5:01	518	5:56	233
4:07	933	5:02	512	5:57	228
4:08	924	5:03	506	5:58	224
4:09	914	5:04	500	5:59	220
4:10	905	5:05	494	6:00	216
4:11	896	5:06	488	6:01	211
4:12	888	5:07	482	6:02	207
4:13	879	5:08	476	6:03	203
4:14	869	5:09	470	6:04	199
4:15	859	5:10	464	6:05	195
4:16	851	5:11	458	6:06	191
4:17	842	5:12	453	6:07	187
4:18	834	5:13	447	6:08	183
4:19	825	5:14	441	6:09	179
4:20	816	5:15	436	6:10	175
4:21	808	5:16	430	6:11	171
4:22	800	5:17	425	6:12	167
4:23	791	5:18	419	6:13	163
4:24	783	5:19	413	6:14	159
4:25	775	5:20	408	6:15	155
4:26	767	5:21	403	6:16	151
4:27	759	5:22	397	6:17	147
4:28	751	5:23	392	6:18	143
4:29	743	5:24	387	6:19	139
4:30	735	5:25	381	6:20	136
4:31	727	5:26	376	6:21	132
4:32	719	5:27	371	6:22	128
4:33	712	5:28	366	6:23	125
4:34	704	5:29	361	6:24	121

(continued)

1,600-Meter Run (continued)

Minutes	Points	Minutes	Points	Minutes	Points
4:35	696	5:30	355	6:25	117
4:36	689	5:31	350	6:26	113
4:37	681	5:32	345	6:27	110
4:38	674	5:33	340	6:28	106
4:39	667	5:34	335	6:29	103
4:40	660	5:35	330	6:30	99
4:41	652	5:36	325	6:31	95
4:42	645	5:37	320	6:32	92
4:43	638	5:38	316	6:33	88
4:44	631	5:39	311		
4:45	624	5:40	306		

Girls' Heptathlon

The girls' heptathlon shall consist of seven events held on two consecutive days in the following order, unless state association rules apply:

First Day

1. 100-meter hurdles (33 inches)
2. High jump
3. Shot put (4 kg)
4. 200-meter dash

Second Day

1. Long jump
2. Javelin throw or discus (depending on state association)
3. 800-meter run

100-Meter Hurdles

Points	Seconds	Points	Seconds	Points	Seconds
12.0	1280	15.4	790	18.8	409
12.1	1264	15.5	777	18.9	400
12.2	1248	15.6	764	19.0	390
12.3	1232	15.7	751	19.1	381
12.4	1216	15.8	739	19.2	372
12.5	1201	15.9	727	19.3	363
12.6	1185	16.0	714	19.4	354
12.7	1170	16.1	702	19.5	345
12.8	1155	16.2	690	19.6	336
12.9	1140	16.3	678	19.7	328
13.0	1124	16.4	666	19.8	319
13.1	1109	16.5	654	19.9	311
13.2	1094	16.6	642	20.0	302
13.3	1080	16.7	631	20.1	294
13.4	1065	16.8	619	20.2	286
13.5	1050	16.9	608	20.3	278
13.6	1036	17.0	596	20.4	270
13.7	1021	17.1	585	20.5	262
13.8	1007	17.2	574	20.6	255
13.9	993	17.3	563	20.7	247
14.0	978	17.4	552	20.8	240
14.1	964	17.5	541	20.9	232
14.2	950	17.6	530	21.0	225
14.3	936	17.7	520	21.1	218
14.4	923	17.8	509	21.2	211
14.5	909	17.9	499	21.3	204
14.6	895	18.0	488	21.4	197
14.7	882	18.1	478	21.5	190
14.8	868	18.2	468	21.6	183
14.9	855	18.3	458	21.7	177
15.0	842	18.4	449	21.8	170
15.1	828	18.5	438	21.9	164
15.2	815	18.6	428	22.0	158
15.3	802	18.7	419		

High Jump

Points	Feet/inches	Meters	Points	Feet/inches	Meters	Points	Feet/inches	Meters
2.09	6' 10"	1359	1.72	5' 7-½"	879	1.35	4' 5"	460
2.08	6' 9-½"	1345	1.71	5' 7"	867	1.34	4' 4-½"	449
2.07	6' 9-¼"	1332	1.70	5' 6-¾"	855	1.33	4' 4"	439
2.06	6' 8-¾"	1318	1.69	5' 6-¼"	842	1.32	4' 3-¾"	429
2.05	6' 8-¼"	1305	1.68	5' 6"	830	1.31	4' 3-¼"	419
2.04	6' 8"	1291	1.67	5' 5-½"	818	1.30	4' 3"	409
2.03	6' 7-½"	1278	1.66	5' 5"	806	1.29	4' 2-½"	399
2.02	6' 7-¼"	1264	1.65	5' 4-¾"	795	1.28	4' 2-¼"	389
2.01	6' 6-¾"	1251	1.64	5' 4-¼"	783	1.27	4' 1-¾"	379
2.00	6' 6-½"	1237	1.63	5' 4"	771	1.26	4' 1-¼"	369
1.99	6' 6"	1224	1.62	5' 3-½"	759	1.25	4' 1"	359
1.98	6' 5-¾"	1211	1.61	5' 3-¼"	747	1.24	4' ½"	350
1.97	6' 5-¼"	1198	1.60	5' 2-¾"	736	1.23	4' ¼"	340
1.96	6' 5"	1184	1.59	5' 2-¼"	724	1.22	3' 11-¾"	331
1.95	6' 4-½"	1171	1.58	5' 2"	712	1.21	3' 11-½"	321
1.94	6' 4-¼"	1158	1.57	5' 1-½"	701	1.20	3' 11"	312
1.93	6' 3-¾"	1145	1.56	5' 1-¼"	689	1.19	3' 10-½"	302
1.92	6' 3-¼"	1132	1.55	5' ¾"	678	1.18	3' 10-¼"	293
1.91	6' 3"	1119	1.54	5' ½"	666	1.17	3' 9-¾"	287
1.90	6' 2-½"	1106	1.53	5' 0"	655	1.16	3' 9-½"	275
1.89	6' 2-¼"	1093	1.52	4' 11-½"	644	1.15	3' 9"	266
1.88	6' 1-¾"	1080	1.51	4' 11-¼"	632	1.14	3' 8-¾"	257
1.87	6' 1-½"	1067	1.50	4' 10-¾"	621	1.13	3' 8-¼"	248
1.86	6' 1"	1054	1.49	4' 10-½"	610	1.12	3' 7-¾"	239
1.85	6' ½"	1041	1.48	4' 10"	599	1.11	3' 7-½"	231
1.84	6' ¼"	1029	1.47	4' 9-¾"	588	1.10	3' 7"	222
1.83	5' 11-¾"	1016	1.46	4' 9-¼"	577	1.09	3' 6-¾"	214
1.82	5' 11-½"	1003	1.45	4' 8-¾"	566	1.08	3' 6-¼"	205
1.81	5' 11"	991	1.44	4' 8-½"	555	1.07	3' 6"	197
1.80	5' 10-½"	978	1.43	4' 8"	544	1.06	5' 5-½"	188
1.79	5' 10-¼"	966	1.42	4' 7-¾"	534	1.05	3' 5"	180
1.78	5' 9-¾"	953	1.41	4' 7-¼"	523	1.04	3' 4-¾"	172
1.77	5' 9-½"	941	1.40	4' 6-¾"	512	1.03	3' 4-¼"	164
1.76	5' 9"	928	1.39	4' 6-½"	502	1.02	3' 4"	156
1.75	5' 8-¾"	916	1.38	4' 6"	491	1.01	3' 3-½"	149
1.74	5' 8-¼"	903	1.37	4' 5-¾"	481	1.00	3' 3-¼"	141
1.73	5' 8"	891	1.36	4' 5-¼"	470			

Shot Put

Meters	Feet/inches	Points	Meters	Feet/inches	Points	Meters	Feet/inches	Points
22.9	75' 1-¼"	1397	17.9	58' 8-½"	1056	12.9	42' 3-¾"	721
22.8	74' 9-¼"	1390	17.8	58' 4-½"	1050	12.8	41' 11-½"	714
22.7	74' 5-½"	1383	17.7	58' ¾"	1043	12.7	41' 7-¾"	708
22.6	74' 1-½"	1377	17.6	57' 8-¾"	1036	12.6	41' 3-¾"	701
22.5	73' 9-½"	1370	17.5	57' 4-¾"	1029	12.5	40' 11-¾"	695
22.4	73' 5-½"	1363	17.4	57' ¾"	1023	12.4	40' 7-¾"	688
22.3	73' 1-¾"	1356	17.3	56' 9"	1016	12.3	40' 4"	681
22.2	72' 9-¾"	1349	17.2	56' 5"	1009	12.2	40' 0"	675
22.1	72' 5-¾"	1342	17.1	56' 1"	1002	12.1	39' 8"	668
22.0	72' 2"	1335	17.0	55' 9-¼"	996	12.0	39' 4-¼"	661
21.9	71' 10"	1329	16.9	55' 5"	989	11.9	39' ¼"	655
21.8	71' 6"	1322	16.8	55' 1"	982	11.8	38' 8-¼"	648
21.7	71' 2-¼"	1315	16.7	54' 9-¼"	975	11.7	38' 4-½"	642
21.6	70' 10-¼"	1308	16.6	54' 5-¼"	969	11.6	38' ½"	635
21.5	70' 6-¼"	1301	16.5	54' 1-¼"	962	11.5	37' 8-½"	628
21.4	70' 2-¼"	1294	16.4	53' 9-¼"	955	11.4	37' 4-½"	622
21.3	69' 10-½"	1288	16.3	53' 5-½"	949	11.3	37' ¾"	615
21.2	69' 6-½"	1281	16.2	53' 1-½"	942	11.2	36' 8-¾"	609
21.1	69' 2-½"	1274	16.1	52' 9-½"	935	11.1	36' 4-¾"	602
21.0	68' 10-¾"	1267	16.0	52' 5-¾"	928	11.0	36' 1"	595
20.9	68' 6-½"	1260	15.9	52' 1-¾"	922	10.9	35' 9"	589
20.8	68' 2-½"	1253	15.8	51' 9-¾"	915	10.8	35' 5"	582
20.7	67' 10-¾"	1247	15.7	51' 6"	908	10.7	35' 1-¼"	576
20.6	67' 6-¾"	1240	15.6	51' 2"	901	10.6	34' 9-¼"	569
20.5	67' 2-¾"	1233	15.5	50' 10"	895	10.5	34' 5-¼"	563
20.4	66' 10-¾"	1226	15.4	50' 6"	888	10.4	34' 1-¼"	556
20.3	66' 7"	1219	15.3	50' 2-¼"	881	10.3	33' 9-¼"	549
20.2	66' 3"	1212	15.2	49' 10-¼"	875	10.2	33' 5-¼"	543
20.1	65' 11"	1206	15.1	49' 6-¼"	868	10.1	33' 1-¼"	536
20.0	65' 7-¼"	1199	15.0	49' 2-½"	861	10.0	32' 9-½"	530
19.9	65' 3-¼"	1192	14.9	48' 10-¼"	855	9.9	32' 5-¼"	523
19.8	64' 11-¼"	1185	14.8	48' 6-¼"	848	9.8	32' 1"	517
19.7	64' 7-½"	1179	14.7	48' 2-½"	841	9.7	31' 9-¼"	510
19.6	64' 3-½"	1172	14.6	47' 10-½"	834	9.6	31' 5-¼"	504
19.5	63' 11-½"	1165	14.5	47' 6-½"	828	9.5	31' 1-½"	497
19.4	63' 7-½"	1158	14.4	47' 2-½"	821	9.4	30' 9-¾"	491
19.3	63' 3-¾"	1151	14.3	46' 10-¾"	814	9.3	30' 6"	484
19.2	62' 11-¾"	1144	14.2	46' 6-¾"	808	9.2	30' 2"	478
19.1	62' 7-¾"	1138	14.1	46' 2-¾"	801	9.1	29' 10"	471
19.0	62' 4"	1131	14.0	45' 11"	794	9.0	29' 6-¼"	465
18.9	61' 11-¾"	1124	13.9	45' 7"	788	8.9	29' 2"	458
18.8	61' 7-¾"	1117	13.8	45' 3"	781	8.8	28' 10"	452
18.7	61' 4"	1111	13.7	44' 11-¼"	774	8.7	28' 6-¼"	445
18.6	61' 0"	1104	13.6	44' 7-¼"	768	8.6	28' 2-¼"	439

(continued)

Shot Put (continued)

Meters	Feet/inches	Points	Meters	Feet/inches	Points	Meters	Feet/inches	Points
18.5	60' 8"	1097	13.5	44' 3-¼"	761	8.5	27' 10-¼"	432
18.4	60' 4"	1090	13.4	43' 11-¼"	754	8.4	27' 6-¼"	426
18.3	60' ¼"	1084	13.3	43' 7-½"	748	8.3	27' 2-½"	419
18.2	59' 8-¼"	1077	13.2	43' 3-½"	741	8.2	26' 10-½"	413
18.1	59' 4-¼"	1070	13.1	42' 11-½"	734	8.1	26' 6-½"	406
18.0	59' ½"	1063	13.0	42' 7-¾"	728	8.0	26' 2-¾"	400

200-Meter Dash

Seconds	Points	Seconds	Points	Seconds	Points
21.5	1234	24.9	896	28.3	608
21.6	1223	25.0	887	28.4	600
21.7	1213	25.1	877	28.5	592
21.8	1202	25.2	869	28.6	584
21.9	1191	25.3	860	28.7	577
22.0	1181	25.4	851	28.8	569
22.1	1171	25.5	842	28.9	560
22.2	1160	25.6	833	29.0	554
22.3	1150	25.7	824	29.1	547
22.4	1140	25.8	815	29.2	539
22.5	1129	25.9	806	29.3	532
22.6	1119	26.0	797	29.4	525
22.7	1109	26.1	789	29.5	518
22.8	1099	26.2	780	29.6	511
22.9	1089	26.3	771	29.7	504
23.0	1079	26.4	763	29.8	496
23.1	1069	26.5	754	29.9	489
23.2	1059	26.6	746	30.0	482
23.3	1049	26.7	737	30.1	475
23.4	1039	26.8	729	30.2	469
23.5	1029	26.9	720	30.3	462
23.6	1019	27.0	712	30.4	455
23.7	1010	27.1	704	30.5	448
23.8	1000	27.2	695	30.6	441
23.9	990	27.3	687	30.7	435
24.0	981	27.4	679	30.8	428
24.1	971	27.5	671	30.9	421
24.2	962	27.6	663	31.0	414
24.3	952	27.7	655	31.1	408
24.4	943	27.8	647	31.2	402
24.5	933	27.9	639	31.3	395
24.6	924	28.0	631	31.4	389
24.7	915	28.1	623	31.5	383
24.8	905	28.2	615	31.5	377

Long Jump

Meters	Feet/inches	Points	Meters	Feet/inches	Points	Meters	Feet/inches	Points
7.4	24' 3"	1309	5.5	18' ¼"	700	3.6	11' 9-½"	220
7.3	23' 11-¼"	1275	5.4	17' 8-¼"	671	3.5	11' 5-½"	200
7.2	23' 7-¼"	1240	5.3	17' 4-½"	643	3.4	11' 1-½"	180
7.1	23' 3-¼"	1206	5.2	17' ½"	614	3.3	10' 9-¾"	161
7.0	22' 11-½"	1172	5.1	16' 8-½"	587	3.2	10' 5-¾"	142
6.9	22' 8-¾"	1139	5.0	16' 4-¾"	559	3.1	10' 1-¾"	124
6.8	22' 4-¾"	1105	4.9	16' ½"	532	3.0	9' 10"	107
6.7	22' 1"	1072	4.8	15' 8-½"	506	2.9	9' 5-¾"	91
6.6	21' 9"	1040	4.7	15' 4-¾"	479	2.8	9' 1-¾"	75
6.5	21' 5"	1007	4.6	15' ¾"	454	2.7	8' 10"	60
6.4	21' 1"	975	4.5	14' 8-¾"	428	2.6	8' 6"	46
6.3	20' 9-¼"	943	4.4	14' 4-¾"	403	2.5	8' 2"	34
6.2	20' 5-¼"	912	4.3	14' 1"	379	2.4	7' 10"	22
6.1	20' 1-¼"	880	4.2	13' 9"	355	2.3	7' 6-¼"	12
6.0	19' 8"	850	4.1	13' 5"	331	2.2	7' 2-¼"	5
5.9	19' 4"	819	4.0	13' 1-¼"	308	2.1	6' 10-¼"	0
5.8	19' 0"	789	3.9	12' 9-¼"	285	2.0	6' 6-½"	0
5.7	18' 8-¼"	759	3.8	12' 5-¼"	263			
5.6	18' 4-¼"	729	3.7	12' 1-½"	242			

Javelin

Meters	Feet/inches	Points	Meters	Feet/inches	Points	Meters	Feet/inches	Points
77	252' 7"	1390	52	170'7"	900	27	88' 6-¾"	421
76	249' 4"	1369	51	167' 3"	880	26	85' 3-½"	402
75	246' 0"	1350	50	164' 0"	861	25	82' ¼"	383
74	242' 9"	1330	49	160' 9"	841	24	78' 8-¾"	364
73	239' 6"	1310	48	157' 5"	822	23	75' 5-½"	345
72	236' 2"	1290	47	154' 2"	803	22	72' 2"	327
71	232' 11"	1271	46	150' 11"	783	21	68' 10-¾"	308
70	229' 7"	1251	45	147' 7"	764	20	65' 7-¼"	290
69	226' 4"	1232	44	144' 4"	745	19	62' 4"	271
68	223' 1"	1212	43	141' 0"	726	18	59' ½"	252
67	219' 9"	1192	42	137' 9"	706	17	55' 9-¼"	234
66	216' 6"	1173	41	134' 6"	687	16	52' 5-¾"	216
65	213' 3"	1153	40	131' 2"	668	15	49' 2-½"	197
64	209' 11"	1133	39	127' 11"	649	14	45' 11"	179
63	206' 8"	1114	38	124' 8"	630	13	42' 7-¾"	161
62	203' 4"	1094	37	121' 4"	610	12	39' 4-¼"	143
61	200' 1"	1075	36	118' 1"	591	11	36' 1"	125
60	196' 10"	1055	35	114' 9"	572	10	32' 9-½"	107
59	193' 6"	1036	34	111' 6"	553	9	29' 6-¼"	89
58	190' 3"	1016	33	105' 3"	534	8	26' 2-¾"	71
57	187' 0"	997	32	104' 11"	515	7	21' 11-½"	54

(continued)

Javelin (continued)

Meters	Feet/inches	Points	Meters	Feet/inches	Points	Meters	Feet/inches	Points
56	183' 8"	977	31	101' 8"	496	6	19' 8"	36
55	180' 5"	958	30	98' 5"	477	5	16' 4-¾"	19
54	177' 1"	938	29	95' 1-½"	458	4	13' 1-¼"	3
53	173' 10"	919	28	91' 10-¼"	439			

800-Meter Run

Time	Points	Time	Points	Time	Points
1:52	1245	2:39	584	3:26	162
1:53	1228	2:40	573	3:27	155
1:54	1212	2:41	561	3:28	149
1:55	1196	2:42	550	3:29	143
1:56	1180	2:43	539	3:30	137
1:57	1164	2:44	528	3:31	131
1:58	1148	2:45	517	3:32	126
1:59	1132	2:46	506	3:33	120
2:00	1116	2:47	495	3:34	115
2:01	1101	2:48	485	3:35	109
2:02	1085	2:49	474	3:36	104
2:03	1070	2:50	464	3:37	99
2:04	1054	2:51	453	3:38	94
2:05	1039	2:52	443	3:39	89
2:06	1024	2:53	433	3:40	84
2:07	1009	2:54	423	3:41	80
2:08	994	2:55	413	3:42	75
2:09	979	2:56	403	3:43	71
2:10	965	2:57	394	3:44	66
2:11	950	2:58	384	3:45	62
2:12	936	2:59	375	3:46	58
2:13	921	3:00	365	3:47	54
2:14	907	3:01	356	3:48	51
2:15	893	3:02	347	3:49	47
2:16	879	3:03	338	3:50	44
2:17	865	3:04	329	3:51	40
2:18	851	3:05	320	3:52	37
2:19	837	3:06	311	3:53	34
2:20	824	3:07	303	3:54	31
2:21	810	3:08	294	3:55	28
2:22	797	3:09	286	3:56	25
2:23	783	3:10	278	3:57	23
2:24	770	3:11	270	3:58	20
2:25	757	3:12	262	3:59	18
2:26	744	3:13	254	4:00	15
2:27	731	3:14	246	4:01	13

(continued)

Time	Points	Time	Points	Time	Points
2:28	718	3:15	238	4:02	11
2:29	705	3:16	231	4:03	10
2:30	693	3:17	223	4:04	8
2:31	680	3:18	216	4:05	6
2:32	668	3:19	209	4:06	5
2:33	656	3:20	202	4:07	4
2:34	644	3:21	195	4:08	3
2:35	632	3:22	188	4:09	2
2:36	620	3:23	181	4:10	1
2:37	608	3:24	174		
2:38	596	3:25	168		

GLOSSARY

Track and Field

clerk of the course—Records the name and number of competitors and assigns them to the proper heat and starting position, as approved by the games committee or meet director.

false start—Occurs when a runner begins a race before the starting pistol is fired. A competitor is disqualified on the first false start.

field referee—Responsible for the conduct and supervision of all field events.

field judge—Officiates the throwing events and jumping events. Individual head field event judges report directly to the field referee.

finish judges—At least two assistant finish judges should be assigned for each place to be scored. The head finish judge views the finish of the race as a whole and designates the place for each assistant finish judge to focus on.

finish-line recorder—Duties revolve around recording times and places. Responsible for recording the official order of finish of all qualifiers or place-winners from results submitted by the head finish judge, recording times as submitted by the head timer, recording anemometer readings when applicable and delivering race results to the official scorer.

fully automatic timing (FAT)—In their championship meets, most state associations use a FAT device that provides a photo or video of the finish of each race.

games committee—The committee responsible for conducting a track and field meet. For dual meets, this committee might consist solely of a meet director or referee; for invitational meets, it usually consists of several people.

heat—Qualifying round, to narrow the field and advance runners to the finals.

hurdle chief—Is usually assisted by 10 to 20 hurdle setters and sets the flight nearest the starting line first so hurdlers can practice starts while remaining hurdles are being set.

jury of appeals—At times, a jury of appeals is appointed for a meet. If this is the case, the jury serves as the final board of appeals. The jury rules in cases when a coach who is protesting a ruling to the referee is not satisfied with the referee's judgment. Often the games committee serves as the jury of appeals.

marshal—The marshal keeps all restricted areas free from unauthorized personnel at all times, giving particular attention to landing areas in the throwing events, jump and vault runways, and starting and finishing areas.

meet director—Often operates as the sole member of the games committee, especially for dual meets. The meet director takes care of the duties that help the meet run smoothly.

meet sanction—If a sanction is required by the state association or the NFHS, the sanction is usually obtained by the meet director at least 30 days prior to the meet.

meet scorer—Records the results from each event at its completion.

photo finish—The term used when a finish is so close that the winner must be determined by a photographic device at the finish line.

records clerk—Is in charge of all clerical work involving meet records.

referee—Is in charge of all activities during a competition and supervises all meet officials.

running referee—Except for the meet referee, the running referee has more jurisdiction over the running events than any other official.

starter—Uses the starting device approved by the games committee: either a voice amplification device or an electronic sound system. Decides, without appeal, whether a start is fair and legal.

surveyor—Inspects and measures the track and all takeoffs and landing pits for the jumps and vaults, the throwing circles for the shot and discus, the foul lines for the javelin and the exchange zones for the relays.

timer—The head timer is in charge of the assistant timers. The head timer is responsible for determining the winning time for each running event and records times for all place-winners as established by the games committee. The head timer or a designated assistant timer calls out lap times in distance races.

umpire—The head umpire supervises the assistant umpires and positions them so they can best carry out their responsibilities. Umpires report race irregularities to the head umpire; the head umpire reports directly to the referee, who makes final decisions.

wind-aided effort—Refers to running events up to and including the 200-meter race, as well as the long jump and triple jump, in which the velocity of the wind exceeds 2 meters per second in the direction of the competition. Records set on a wind-aided effort are not allowed.

wind gauge operator—Reads wind velocities to validate record performance in events up to and including 200 meters plus the long and triple jumps.

Cross Country

caller—Calls the number of each runner in the order of his or her proper place in the chute.

checker—Keeps a record of the runners and their order of the finish as announced by the caller.

chute director—Supervises the finish chute, which includes directing gate controllers when more than one chute is used, directing marshals to keep the chute area free of unauthorized individuals and assigning positions for chute umpires and any other necessary personnel.

chute umpire—Supervises runners after they enter the chute and ensures they're properly checked to prevent any irregularity in the order of finish. The chute umpire ensures that all runners who cross the finish line are given their proper order as they progress through the chute.

clerk of the course—Places the teams in proper position on the starting line.

course umpire—Observes runners during the race. If any runner fails to run the proper course or otherwise violates the rules, the umpires report the infraction to the referee.

finish judge—Stands outside the chute and on the finish line to determine the proper order in which competitors enter the chute.

marshal—Keeps the competitive area free of all individuals except officials, runners and other individuals authorized by the games committee.

meet director—The individual most responsible for scheduling and preparing for a meet.

referee—Disqualifies any competitor for unsporting conduct or any violation of the rules.

timer—Records the called-out times of all runners who finish the race. Timers can also be assigned to designated positions along the course to call out elapsed time to runners during the race.

INDEX

Note: The italicized *f* and *t* following page numbers refer to figures and tables, respectively.

ABOUT THE AUTHOR

Officiating Track & Field and Cross Country was written by the American Sport Education Program (ASEP) in cooperation with the National Federation of State High School Associations (NFHS). Based in Indianapolis, the NFHS is the rules authority for high school sports in the United States. Hundreds of thousands of officials nationwide and worldwide rely on the NFHS for officiating guidance. ASEP is a division of Human Kinetics, Inc., based in Champaign, Illinois, and has been a world leader in providing educational courses and resources to professional and volunteer coaches, officials, parents, and sport administrators for more than 20 years. ASEP and the NFHS have teamed up to offer books, CDs and online courses for high school officials through the NFHS Officials Education Program.

NFHS Officials Education Program

ONLINE EDUCATION FOR ON-THE-GO OFFICIALS

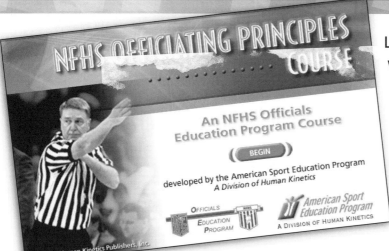

Late-night games.
Weekend tournaments.
Pregame preparation.
Postgame reflection.
As an official, just because you keep track of time doesn't mean you have any. So instead of taking even more time out to attend another officials clinic, explore the timesaving, schedule-friendly online courses offered through the **NFHS Officials Education Program.**

A joint effort between the **National Federation of State High School Associations (NFHS)** and the **American Sport Education Program (ASEP)**, the NFHS Officials Education Program features a two-part, Internet-delivered curriculum covering officiating principles and sport-specific methods based on NFHS rules.

Available now is ***NFHS Officiating Principles,*** a course applicable to all officials regardless of their sport. The course shows you how to determine your officiating philosophy and style, improve communication, develop decision-making skills, manage conflict, understand legal responsibilities, manage your officiating career, and much more.

Coming soon: ***Officiating [Sport] Methods*** courses for softball, football, soccer, basketball, wrestling, and baseball cover the sport-specific methods and mechanics of officiating as they apply to NFHS rules and regulations. The officiating [sport] book that you have in your hands serves as the text for the course. Check the ASEP Web site at www.ASEP.com for updates on course availability.

NFHS Officials Education Program offers you the continuing education you need as an official on a schedule that's right for you. Registration fees are only $75 per course and include a course text, CD-ROM, study guide, exam, and entry into the National Officials Registry. For more information, or to register for a course, visit **www.ASEP.com** or call ASEP at **800-747-5698.**